GREAT AIRCRAFT OF WWII
P-51 MUSTANG
AND
B-17 FLYING FORTRESS

GREAT AIRCRAFT OF WWII
P-51 MUSTANG
AND
B-17 FLYING FORTRESS

Abbeydale Press

This paperback edition published in 2007 by
Abbeydale Press
An imprint of Bookmart Ltd
Registered Number 2372865
Blaby Road, Wigston,
Leicestershire, LE18 4SE
United Kingdom

ISBN 978-1-86147-214-4

1 3 5 7 9 10 8 6 4 2

Originally published in 1997 by Bookmart Ltd as part of
Great Aircraft of WWII

Cover design: Omnipress Ltd, Eastbourne, UK
Cover images: © David Wall / Alamy, © Antony Nettle / Alamy

Printed in Singapore

CONTENTS

'The Forts were dropping their bombs, but the sky was so black with flak that we could only occasionally see them as they flew through the solid wall of sooty explosions. Don was the first to see the Me 109.

'"Johnny, at six o'clock high there's a single bandit."

'I looked back, and there he was, high above us. I gazed in disbelief as his nose dropped and he plummeted down on us.

'"Don, the crazy son of a bitch is bouncing us."

'"I know. When I yell 'Break', you break right and I'll break left."

'I watched as the 109 dropped closer and closer. "Break, Johnny."

'I pulled sharply to the right, and thought at first I had broken too late as the 109 pulled onto my tail. I tightened my turn and met Don halfway around as he tried to fire on the 109 in a head-on attack. I went around twice more with the Jerry on my tail before Don could reverse his turn and swing down for a rear attack. But this German pilot was a smart, capable flyer. As Don brought his guns to bear, he Split-S and dove to the ground. Don and I followed him, our motors roaring in pursuit. He pulled out of his dive and banked left, which brought him close to

me. I followed him and fired. He wasn't one to sit still, however, and changed his turn to swing into Don. I followed, firing intermittently. Don meanwhile had climbed for altitude, and I kept the Jerry busy in a tight turn. As I fired, I saw flashes on his wing, fuselage, and even his motor, but the pilot wouldn't bale out. Turning all the time and losing height, we were now just above the tree tops, and the 109's engine was spewing smoke. I had no forewarning that my ammunition was running out, but as I prepared for the final burst, only silence came as I pressed the tit.

'"Finish him, Don, I'm out of ammunition."

'Don, who had been maneuvring above us waiting for the Jerry to break out of the turn, zoomed down in front of me and made one pass on the courageous German flyer. His shots hit home . . .'

■ COMBAT DUO ■

The two Mustang pilots in this successful combat were two of America's finest; Don Gentile (21 victories) and John T. Godfrey (18 victories). Members of the 336th Fighter Squadron, 4th Fighter Group in the spring of 1944, the deadly duo became legendary for their teamwork, even though they only flew as a pair on five occasions.

This combat was notable on several counts. The Me 109G opposing them was in many ways the equal of the Mustang, and it started the combat with the dual advantages of height and position. The German pilot showed great confidence in engaging after it became clear that the element of surprise had been lost, when the safe move would have been to disengage and climb away, using the excess speed generated in his attacking dive. As it was, he was evidently banking on disposing of Godfrey before

Left: Probably the greatest exponents of air combat teamwork in the USAAF were Captain Don Gentile, seen here in the cockpit of his P-51B *Shangri-La*, and Lieutenant John Godfrey, perched on the wing wearing flying helmet, goggles and Mae West (10 April 1944). On return to the USA, Gentile became an Air Force test pilot (KIFA 28 Jan 1951); Godfrey returned to action in August, was shot down by ground fire later that month, and became a prisoner of war (died 12 June 1958). (USAF)

GENTILE AND GODFREY VERSUS ME 109

(1) the two Mustangs break in opposite directions, The Me 109 follows Godfrey's hard turn. (2) Gentile opens fire, misses, then turns away to reposition. Meanwhile Godfrey flies tight circles to deny the Messerschmit a shot. Gentile gets behind the German (3), who tries to disengage with a vertical dive (4) with Gentile in pursuit. Godfrey, now free, also dives to cut the 109 off (5). The German pilot pulls out of his dive (6) and turns towards Godfrey, but with Gentile still on his tail is forced to turn away. With Godfrey in an attacking position, Gentile pulls up and circles (7). Godfrey runs out of ammunition and calls Gentile, who dives and delivers a lethal burst (8).

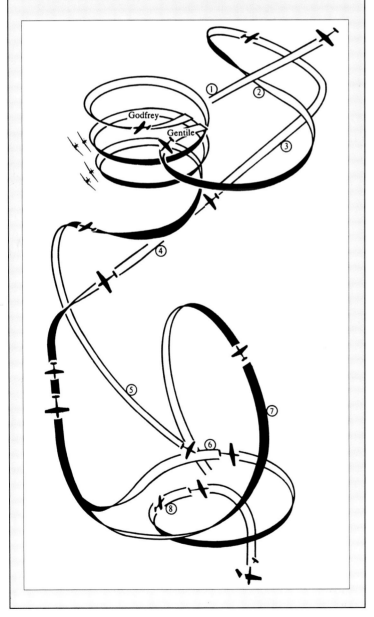

Gentile could intervene, then taking on the second Mustang in a one-versus-one combat.

That he failed was due to the excellence of the P-51B, which turned hard enough to deny him a valid shooting opportunity, and the skill of John Godfrey in holding him off until Gentile could take up an attacking position.

Having lost the initiative, and outnumbered two to one, he attempted to disengage with a near-vertical dive to ground level. The superb performance of the two Mustangs allowed them to follow him down with relative ease, with Gentile in hot pursuit. Even then he might still have escaped had it not been for the teamwork of the two Mustang pilots, one of whom held him in play while the other jockeyed for position, the leadership passing back and forth between them as opportunity offered. But against what was acknowledged to be the best fighting pair in the USAAF, flying aircraft fully the equal of his own, his bravery and flying skills availed him nothing.

■ PRECISION BOMBING RAIDS ■

When the United States of America entered the war, their policy in Europe was to carry out precision bombing raids on selected targets. The main bomber type was the Boeing B-17 Flying Fortress, which not only had adequate range for the task, but carried very heavy defensive armament. In theory this would allow the bombers, flying in close formation, to beat off massed attacks by German fighters. In practice this did not work at all well. With shallow penetrations of enemy airspace, casualties were sustainable, as the time spent in the combat area was limited. However, with deep penetrations the German fighter arm was able to react in force over a considerable period, and US losses rose to unacceptable levels.

The only possible answer was to match fighters with fighters, but there were problems. Single-seat, single-engined fighters of the time were traditionally short-legged, while the longer-ranged twin-engined fighters were outclassed by agile enemy single-engined fighters. Germany had learned this lesson during the Battle of Britain, when the Me 110 took a series of heavy beatings from the nimble British Spitfires and Hurricanes. Somehow a single-seater, single-engined agile fighter with the required range had to be found.

The solution came in the unlikely shape of an American airframe initially developed for the RAF, married to the outstanding Rolls-Royce Merlin engine. The Mustang had almost double the fuel capacity of the Spitfire and a correspondingly greater radius of action. On late models, the addition of a large fuel tank in the fuselage and two drop tanks under the wings increased the range to the point where the American fighter could rove the length and breadth of the Third Reich. Wherever the bombers went, Mustangs could accompany them, to the dismay and discomfiture of the defending German fighters.

■ MERLIN ENGINE ■

The Merlin engine had been adopted to provide the high-altitude performance lacking in the original Allison-engined aircraft. That the airframe was good there was no doubt; the early model Mustang had proved itself to be an outstanding fighter at low and medium altitudes. The RAF used it in roles where high-altitude performance was not required, such as ground attack, army co-operation and low-level reconnaissance.

The USAAF was not slow to follow suit, with the attack version redesignated the A-36 Invader and the tactical reconnaissance aircraft the F-6. The fighter variant was at first known as the Apache in USAAF service; only later were both names abandoned in favour of Mustang, which, already used by the British, in the long run saved a lot of confusion.

While the Merlin-engined Mustang variants were by far the most important of the breed, and the type

Above: Wherever there was action, Mustangs were sure to be found. They ranged Europe from Norway in the north to Italy in the south, and from France in the west to Russia in the east. North African deserts, Burmese jungles, Chinese paddy fields, the vast wastes of the Pacific, even the skies over Japan – all heard the thunder of their engines. (Arvin Williams via JE)

gained undying fame in the skies of Western Europe, it was used in virtually every theatre of operations during the Second World War. A handful of Mustangs was supplied to the Soviet Union, although these were far too few to have any real impact. B-17 Fortresses on the so-called 'Shuttle' missions, which flew on to Russian bases after bombing Germany, were accompanied by Mustangs, which sometimes operated briefly on the Eastern Front. Mustangs were also based in southern Italy, from where they could range as far afield as Romania, Bavaria, or the south of France.

In the Far East, the Japanese were made well aware of the presence of the P-51, units of which were at various times based in India, Burma and China. Even in the vast Pacific Ocean, traditionally the domain of the US Navy carrier fleets, the Mustang's immense radius of action was put to good use. Based on Iwo Jima towards the end of the war, Mustangs escorted the huge B-29 Superfortresses during raids on the Japanese home islands.

Like all fighters of the era, the Mustang underwent a process of continuous development, and its performance started to approach the limits of what was possible with the internal combustion engine and not very efficient propeller. The other limit which had been pushed very hard indeed was pilot endurance. After a seven-hour mission over Germany, a pilot was completely exhausted. The

Below: The combination of the British Rolls-Royce Merlin engine and the American P-51 Mustang airframe resulted in a superb fighter. With the addition of extra fuel tanks, it was able to escort the heavy bombers over previously unheard-of distances.

answer had to be a second pilot to share the load. But how was this to be done without compromising performance?

The answer was the P-82 Twin Mustang. In essence, two Mustang fuselages and tails were coupled together with a central wing and tail section, with the outboard wings remaining unchanged. This gave two cockpits, while range and performance remained largely unimpaired; only manoeuvrability suffered, and that not to any great degree. Still later an airborne interception radar was fitted, giving night and all-weather Twin Mustangs.

■ KOREA ■

The end of the Second World War coincided with the emergence of the new breed of jet fighters. Totally outperformed, the Mustang seemed as if its days as a front line combat aircraft were numbered. It had, however, one remaining advantage. Early jet engines were incredibly thirsty, and their acceleration was sluggish. Consequently endurance was almost non-existent by comparison with the Mustang, and they were unable to use short temporary airstrips from which the piston-engined fighter could operate with ease.

This endurance was to show to advantage in the war in Korea, which broke out in 1950. Japan-based jets could stay over the battle area for just a few minutes, whereas P-82s from the same base could loiter for much longer, and P-51s could be based 'in-country'. The final combat sortie of an American

Below: 1945 saw the Mustang the dominant fighter in the USAAF, but it was outclassed and superseded by the new jet fighters, typically the Lockheed P-80 Shooting Star shown here. (Author)

P-51 took place from Korea in January 1953, but this was far from the final combat mission to be flown.

Above: Even in 1944, the German Me 262 jet gave the Mustang a hard time in combat. A far greater mismatch nearly occurred in 1963. If the confrontation between Malaysia and Indonesia had resulted in open war, Indonesian Mustangs would have had to face missile-armed Mach 2 Lightnings of the RAF. (BAe via author)

Israeli Mustangs flew in defence of the newly formed state from late 1948, and even in 1956 they took an important, if secondary, role in the Suez war before being phased out during the following year. In 1963, a confrontation took place between Malaysia and Indonesia. The main Indonesian fighter type was the Mustang. The air defence of Malaysia was largely in the hands of the Royal Air Force, equipped with the Mach 2-capable Lightning. In the event of overt hostilities, this would have been a tremendous mismatch; perhaps fortunately for the Indonesian fighter pilots it did not occur. Finally, in what was perhaps the most ridiculous war ever, Salvadorean Mustangs fought with Honduran Corsairs and Thunderbolts. This was the combat swansong of the Mustang, which was soon after relegated to airshows and unlimited-class racing.

In what was to prove a final renaissance for the fighter, the Cavalier Aircraft Corporation PA-48 Enforcer made its maiden flight on 9 April 1983. A heavily modified Mustang, it was offered to the South American market as a light tactical aircraft. There were no takers, and the programme was finally terminated in 1986. The Mustang is long gone from the military scene, but its proud legend lives on. This is its story.

NORTH AMERICAN P-51B MUSTANG

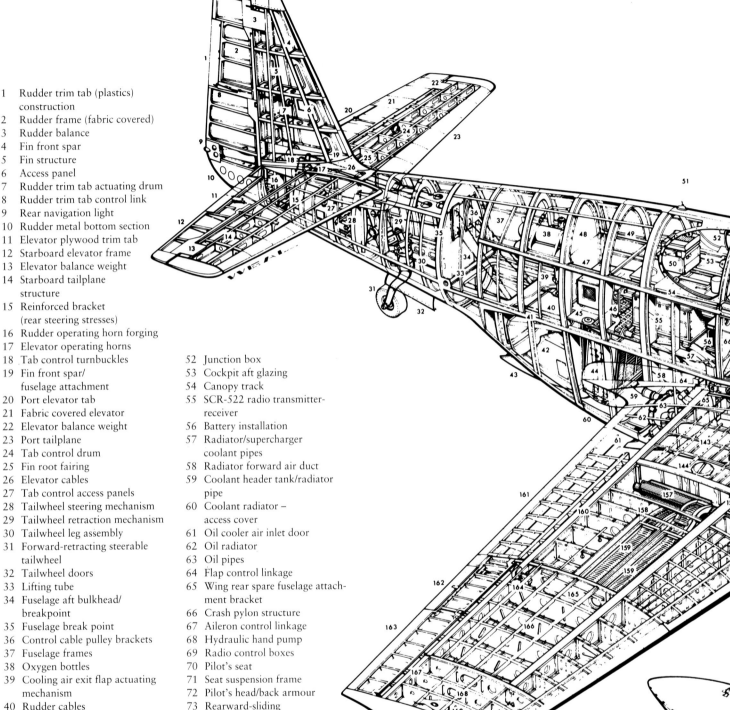

1 Rudder trim tab (plastics) construction
2 Rudder frame (fabric covered)
3 Rudder balance
4 Fin front spar
5 Fin structure
6 Access panel
7 Rudder trim tab actuating drum
8 Rudder trim tab control link
9 Rear navigation light
10 Rudder metal bottom section
11 Elevator plywood trim tab
12 Starboard elevator frame
13 Elevator balance weight
14 Starboard tailplane structure
15 Reinforced bracket (rear steering stresses)
16 Rudder operating horn forging
17 Elevator operating horns
18 Tab control turnbuckles
19 Fin front spar/ fuselage attachment
20 Port elevator tab
21 Fabric covered elevator
22 Elevator balance weight
23 Port tailplane
24 Tab control drum
25 Fin root fairing
26 Elevator cables
27 Tab control access panels
28 Tailwheel steering mechanism
29 Tailwheel retraction mechanism
30 Tailwheel leg assembly
31 Forward-retracting steerable tailwheel
32 Tailwheel doors
33 Lifting tube
34 Fuselage aft bulkhead/ breakpoint
35 Fuselage break point
36 Control cable pulley brackets
37 Fuselage frames
38 Oxygen bottles
39 Cooling air exit flap actuating mechanism
40 Rudder cables
41 Ruselage lower longeron
42 Rear tunnel
43 Cooling air exit flap
44 Coolant radiator assembly
45 Radio and equipment shelf
46 Power supply pack
47 Fuselage upper longeron
48 Radio bay aft bulkhead (plywood)
49 Fuselage stringers
50 SCR-695 radio transmitter-receiver (on upper sliding shelf)
51 Whip aerial

52 Junction box
53 Cockpit aft glazing
54 Canopy track
55 SCR-522 radio transmitter-receiver
56 Battery installation
57 Radiator/supercharger coolant pipes
58 Radiator forward air duct
59 Coolant header tank/radiator pipe
60 Coolant radiator – access cover
61 Oil cooler air inlet door
62 Oil radiator
63 Oil pipes
64 Flap control linkage
65 Wing rear spare fuselage attachment bracket
66 Crash pylon structure
67 Aileron control linkage
68 Hydraulic hand pump
69 Radio control boxes
70 Pilot's seat
71 Seat suspension frame
72 Pilot's head/back armour
73 Rearward-sliding clear-vision canopy
74 External rear-view mirror
75 Ring and bead gunsight
76 Bullet-proof windshield
77 Gyroscopic gunsight
78 Engine controls
79 Signal pistol discharge tube
80 Circuit-breaker panel
81 Oxygen regulator
82 Pilot's foot-rest and seat mounting bracket
83 Control linkage
84 Rudder pedal

85 Tailwheel lock control
86 Wing centre-section
87 Hydraulic reservoir
88 Port wing fuel tank filler point
89 Port 0.5in (12.7mm) machine guns
90 Ammunition feed chutes

91 Gun bay access door (raised)
92 Ammunition box troughs
93 Aileron control cables
94 Flap lower skin (Alclad)
95 Aileron profile (internal aero-dynamic balance diaphragm)
96 Aileron control drum and

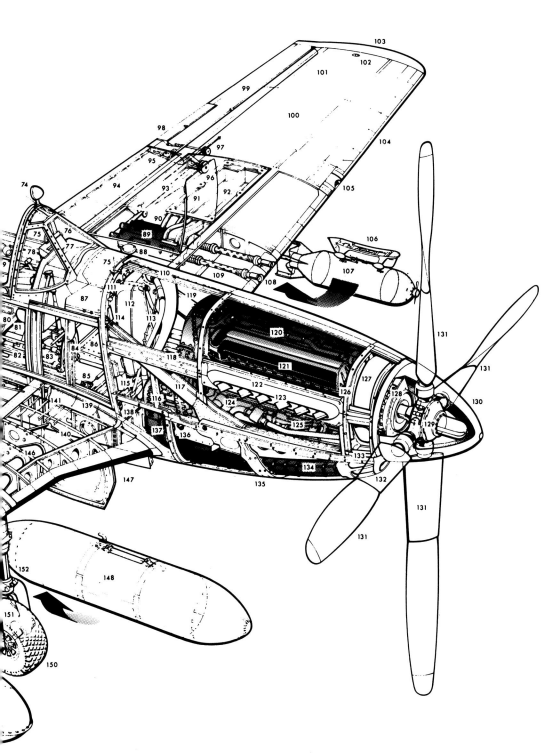

115 Oil tank metal retaining straps
116 Carburettor
117 Engine bearer assembly
118 Cowling panel frames
119 Engine altercooler
120 Engine leads
121 Packard (Rolls-Royce Merlin) V-1650 engine
122 Exhaust fairing panel
123 Stub exhausts
124 Magneto
125 Coolant pipes
126 Cowling forward frame
127 Coolant header tank
128 Armour plate
129 Propeller hub
130 Spinner
131 Four-blade Hamilton Standard Hydromatic propeller
132 Carburettor air intake, integral with 133
133 Engine mount front frame assembly
134 Intake trunking
135 Engine mount reinforcing tie
136 Hand crank starter
137 Carburettor/trunking vibration-absorbing connection
138 Wing centre-section front bulk-head
139 Wing centre-section end rib
140 Starboard mainwheel well
141 Wing front spar/fuselage attach-ment bracket
142 Ventral air intake (radiator and oil cooler assemblies)
143 Starboard wing fuel tank
144 Fuel filler point
145 Mainwheel leg mount/pivot
146 Mainwheel leg rib cut-outs
147 Main gear fairing doors
148 Auxiliary fuel tank (plastic/ pressed paper composition); capacity 90 Imp gal (409l)
149 Auxiliary fuel tank (metal) capacity 62 gal (284 litres)
150 27in (68.6cm) smooth-contour mainwheel
151 Axle fork
152 Towing lugs
153 Landing gear fairing
154 Main gear shock strut
155 Blast tubes
156 Wing front spar
157 Gun bay
158 Ammunition feed chutes
159 Ammunition boxes
160 Wing rear spar
161 Flap structure
162 Starboard aileron tab
163 Starboard aileron
164 Starboard aileron tab adjustment mechanism (ground setting)
165 Wing rib strengthening
166 Outboard section structure
167 Outer section single spar
168 Wingtip sub-assembly
169 Starboard navigation light
170 Detachable wingtip

mounting bracket
97 Aileron trim tab control drum
98 Aileron trim tab plastics (phenol fibre) construction
99 Port aileron assembly
100 Wing skinning
101 Outer section sub-assembly
102 Port navigation light
103 Port wingtip
104 Leading-edge skin
105 Landing lamp
106 Weapons/stores pylon
107 500lb (227kg) bomb
108 Gun ports
109 Machine gun barrels
110 Detachable cowling panels
111 Firewall/integral armour
112 Oil tank
113 Oil pipes
114 Upper longeron/engine mount attachment

BIRTH OF A FIGHTER

With war looming in the late Thirties, it became a matter of urgency for Britain and France to expand their air forces. With their home industries already heavily committed, it was only natural that they should turn to the United States.

The best of the American fighters of this period was the Curtiss P-40. The prototype of this had first flown in the autumn of 1938, more than two years after the Spitfire, but it was in fact little more than a re-engined Hawk 75 of rather earlier vintage. A large production order for the US Army Air Corps was placed in May 1939, and this meant that the manufacturers had little spare capacity to meet export orders for Britain and France in the immediate future. At this stage, the British Purchasing Commission, based in New York, sought a second-source manufacturer. Their choice lighted on North American Aviation, based at Inglewood, California.

At that time, North American was mainly noted for its NA-16 Harvard trainer, and its sole experience of fighter design consisted of a handful of NA-50s and NA-68s for Thailand. These were in essence Harvards with more powerful engines and armament. This notwithstanding, the idea of licence-production of the Curtiss fighter did not really appeal to North American. Studies for a new fighter had been underway since the previous summer, and these appeared to indicate that the company could design a fighter around the same Allison engine used by the P-40, but which would have far better performance than the Curtiss.

A proposal was made to the British in January 1940, which resulted in a contract for a prototype, designated

Left: Prior to the P-51, North American Aviation lacked experience in fighter design, its previous attempt in this field being a souped-up and armed version of the T-6 trainer, two of which are seen here with the Mustang prototype.

Below left: The NA-73X prototype. Sleek but angular, it was vaguely similar in appearance to the German Messerschmitt Me 109E, which gave rise to all sorts of unfounded rumours. From this angle, the wingtip shows the approximate configuration of the laminar flow section that was to play such a tremendous part in the Mustang's success. (AAHS via JE)

Far left: The instrument panel of the early Mustangs was tidily laid out, as can be seen in this photograph taken during assembly, although it followed American rather than British practice. Another departure from British practice was the wrap-around perspex windshield, with an armoured glass screen behind it. If the windshield misted up, as frequently happened, the pilot was unable to reach past the armoured glass to wipe it. The answer was a revised windshield with an armoured glass panel incorporated; this was implemented on the second production batch. Also visible here are the reflector sight and the rearview mirror. (Roger Freeman)

NA-73X. Part of the mythology of the Mustang's origins was that the British insisted that the new fighter should be produced from scratch in just four months. In fact, this arose from a statement by NAA President Dutch Kindelberger, but it was never an element in the contract. Of course, the dice were loaded; design studies had, as we have seen, been underway for almost a year, and when the contract was signed on 23 May 1940, much of the detail design was already complete. It was however a remarkable achievement that the NA-73X was rolled out just 102 days later, even though it lacked an engine and the wheels had been borrowed from a Harvard!

The NA-73X was sleek but angular. For ease of production, curves were never used where a straight line would do. This gave the aircraft a superficial resemblance to the Me 109E and thus started the canard that NAA designer Edgar Schmued was a German who had once worked on the Messerschmitt fighter. There was of course no truth in this, even though it was to appear in print many times.

One crucial decision was to use a laminar flow wing

Aerodynamic drag increases in direct proportion to the square of the speed; i.e. drag at 400mph is 16 times greater than the drag for the same aircraft at 100mph. The only way to obtain greatly improved performance over another fighter which uses the same engine is to substantially reduce drag, and NAA designers made every attempt to do this. At the same time they made every effort to keep weight down by making many items serve more than one purpose.

One of the really critical decisions was to use a laminar flow wing. This had been researched by the National Advisory Committee for Aeronautics (NACA, the forerunner of the modern NASA). The normal aerofoil sections for

DESIGN CONSIDERATIONS

Strictly for comparative purposes, we are including results of a study showing the difference in size and performance between the airplane offered and one which might be offered with a minimum of armament and without protective armor. This second design (P-509) incorporates only four machine guns and is not fitted with protective armor, but is otherwise the same. It will be noted that the high-speed in this condition is 400mph with a wing area of 190 sq. ft. With a full complement of armament and armor plate protection front and rear, the weight is increased from 6,450 lbs to 7,765 lbs and the wing area is increased from 190 sq. ft. to 230 sq. ft. in order to maintain the same landing speed. The resulting performance is materially reduced and the high-speed is 384mph under the same conditions.

EXTRACT FROM LETTER FROM NAA, 1 MAY 1940

the period had their maximum thickness at roughly 20 per cent of the chord, the chord being the distance from front to back. They also had a distinct camber, with a convex upper surface and a concave lower surface. After the airflow passed the thickest point, it had a tendency to 'burble', or become turbulent. The thickest point on a laminar flow wing was more than half-way across the chord, and for all practical purposes it had no camber; both surfaces were convex in shape. In practice this meant that the air tended to slip smoothly past both surfaces, giving a tremendous reduction in drag. There was of course a price to be paid for this; the lift generated was not as high as a more conventional aerofoil section, and for low speeds, large and powerful slotted flaps were needed.

■ ALLISON ENGINE ■

The NA-73X was of all-metal stressed skin construction. The wings, which had pronounced dihedral, contained a sheet-web main spar, and an almost equally strong rear spar, which carried the ailerons and flaps. The distance between spars was sufficient to fit the length of the 0.50in (12.7mm) Browning machine gun, leaving only the barrel to project ahead of the main spar. The main gear legs were widely spaced, giving excellent ground handling, and retracted inwards towards the centreline. The main gear wheels were large, and to house them within the wing, the leading edge was kinked forward inboard to increase wing depth at this point. To minimize drag, the tail wheel was also retractable.

The only engine considered was the Allison V-1710, which was a liquid-cooled 12 cylinder inline producing 1,150hp. Contrary to popular legend, it had a geared supercharger, but power, and with it performance, fell away rapidly above 15,000ft (4,570m). At that time the USAAC had no requirement for high-altitude combat fighters, and all American fighters of the era were equally limited. Even as the NA-73X was being built, combat experience in Europe was proving otherwise, but while a turbo-supercharger was briefly considered, it was discounted at this stage. Traditional engine mountings of the day consisted of a frame of welded steel tubes. NAA differed in designing cantilevered beams, with the engine itself resting on rubber blocks to damp out vibration.

Location of the radiator beneath the fuselage

Another attempt to minimize drag involved the cooling system. Heat from the engine was led to a radiator which dissipated it into the passing air. Heat is of course a form of energy which, unless some means could be found to harness it, was wasted. Theoreticians on both sides of the Atlantic suggested that if the heated air was discharged rearwards at high pressure it could actually provide a small increment of thrust, which in turn would partially offset the drag of the

Left: **A slow flypast by a Mustang I of No. 4 Squadron RAF, using 40 degrees of flap. From this angle, the large flap area is clearly visible. (Roger Freeman)**

Right: Fitting Browning 0.50in (12.7mm) guns and their ammunition feeds in the wings could initially only be done by canting them on their sides, as seen here. This frequently caused jams when they were fired during hard manoeuvres. (Roger Freeman)

Left: The Allison engine installation, showing the carburettor intake. The heavy machine guns mounted low on each side of the engine, together with their synchronization gear, ammunition tanks and feeds, made servicing difficult, and these were deleted on later models. (Roger Freeman)

installation. It demanded great care in designing the ducting for the intake and efflux, with moveable flaps to adjust the flow as necessary. While the principle was well known, early Mustang radiators did not produce thrust in this manner, and only later was this developed.

The optimum location for the radiator installation was found to be beneath the fuselage, just aft of the cockpit. A small penalty was paid in weight for the extra piping required, but in terms of performance it paid off. Not considered at that time was the danger of extra combat vulnerability, but even if this had been taken into account, it would probably have been deemed to be compensated for by increased performance.

■ 8MM SEAT ARMOUR ■

The controls were well harmonized, and instead of cables, which could slacken slightly, adversely affecting handling, the control runs were rods, again at a slight weight penalty. The control surfaces on the tail were fabric-covered, whereas the ailerons were aluminium.

The cockpit was roomy by British standards, with 8mm back armour to protect the pilot. To minimize drag, it was set low, and the roof line was faired into the fuselage. The view 'out of the window' was good, although, as with many contemporary fighters, rearward visibility could have been better. However, the canopy design drew adverse comments from some quarters. Whereas British fighters had sliding hoods, the canopy of the NA-73X was hinged. The panel on the left opened out and downwards, while the roof hinged open to the right. It could not be opened in flight, unlike the British-style canopies, although in an emergency it could be jettisoned. In this it was not unlike the Me 109.

The NA-73X carried no armament, although dummy gun ports were painted on the leading edges of the wings. The proposed armament was heavy by any standards. Two 0.50in (12.7mm) Browning machine guns were mounted

Above: **Test pilot Paul Balfour came to grief on the fifth flight of NA-73X, when the engine cut. His forced landing in a culti-vated field was a disaster, as can be seen here. Damage was extensive, and over seven weeks passed before the aircraft could be flown again.**

low on the nose, synchronized to fire through the propeller. These were staggered to allow their magazines to fit one behind the other. Two more 0.50in (12.7mm) Brownings were set outboard in the wings, with four 0.30in (7.62mm) Brownings further out. The magazines for the wing guns, holding two hundred 0.50in (12.7mm) rounds each or five hundred 0.30in (7.62mm) rounds each, were set well outboard, and fed by conveyor chutes.

The United States being a far larger country than Britain, Americans are perhaps more distance-conscious than their trans-Atlantic cousins. This showed in the design fuel capacity of the NA-73X, which consisted of two 75 imperial gallon (90 US gallon/341 litre) tanks in the inboard wing sections. This was three-quarters as much again as the normal capacity of the Spitfire, and gave the new fighter the remarkable endurance of about four hours.

Fuel capacity – two 75 imperial gallon tanks in the wings

Although the airframe had been rolled out early in September 1940, Allison engines, also used in the P-38, P-39 and P-40, were in short supply. Not until early October did one become available. It was fitted quickly, and taxiing trials commenced. Then, on 26 October,

freelance test pilot Vance Breese lifted the new aircraft off the Mines Field runway for its first flight.

Three more successful test flights were made, which revealed only minor snags apart from a tendency of the engine to overheat. Modifications to the radiator inlet were needed, but before these could be put in hand, near-disaster struck.

On 20 November, company test pilot Paul Balfour took the NA-73X aloft on its fifth test flight. As he approached the runway he throttled back, and as speed bled off the engine started to run roughly, then spluttered to a stop. With no power available, Balfour attempted a dead-stick landing in a cultivated field short of the runway. He selected gear down but, given the soft surface, this was an error. The wheels dug in and the aircraft nosed over onto its back. That there was no fire was fortunate on two counts. Balfour was trapped in the cockpit, the canopy of which was half-buried

Above: **The first production aircraft, AG 345, in British markings. The short carburettor scoop has yet to be lengthened. The nose guns can be seen projecting, while some idea of the unorthodox layout of the wing guns is given by the vertically staggered ports, with the centre guns set lower than the others.**

in the soft earth, and had to be dug free. Secondly, the precious prototype, although damaged, was repairable, and was returned to the flight test programme on 11 January 1941.

One of the more obvious modifications concerned the carburettor scoop. Due to the layout of the Allison engine, this was located on top of the engine cowling. Under certain flight conditions, low airspeed, low revs and increased angle of attack, air ram recovery was insufficient. This had been responsible for the crash of the first prototype. The cure for it was to extend the intake forward to the very front of the cowling.

Ultimately the incident did not jeopardize the project. The urgency of the British requirement meant that the North American fighter had been purchased 'off the drawing board', an order for 320 having been placed in August 1940, following the original letter of intent of 11 April. Then, during December of that year, it was officially named Mustang by the British.

The first production aircraft was scheduled for delivery in January 1941, but, due to various problems, it did not take to the air

until 23 April. This machine was not delivered to the RAF; instead it was retained as a development aircraft by NAA, who flew it intensively in conjunction with the prototype.

■ FIRST MUSTANG ■ IN THE UK

The first Mustang to reach Britain arrived at Liverpool docks in a crate in October 1941, having survived the attentions of the U-boats en route. It was taken to Speke airport, where it was assembled, and made its first flight in its adoptive country on 24 October. From Speke it went to the Aeroplane and Armament Experimental Establishment at Boscombe Down where all operational equipment, British gunsights, radios etc. were installed, and evaluation began. Further evaluation of this aircraft and one other was made by the Air Fighting

Left: **The first production Mustang flew on 23 April 1941. From this angle, the short carburettor scoop above the engine and the radiator housing beneath the fuselage can clearly be seen. The control surfaces on the tail were fabric-covered, which accounts for the different colour. (Paul Coggan via JE).**

FLYING REPORT

The aircraft is pleasant to fly, being extremely stable in all planes. The take-off is rather long, but with little tendency to swing, and as the engine is not fitted with an automatic boost control, care must be taken not to overboost. The landing is easy though the run is longer than taken by a Hurricane or Spitfire. The controls are well balanced and can be made light or heavy as required by adjustment of the servo-tabs fitted to ailerons and elevators. There is little tendency to heavy-up at high speeds. With the controls lightened by the tabs, the Mustang is as light as the Spitfire but far smoother in all manoeuvres. The aircraft handles extremely well in aerobatics and gives ample warning of the stall. In particular, it was found far more difficult to effect a high speed stall than in a Spitfire.

EXTRACT AFDU REPORT 5.5.42.

Development Unit at RAF Duxford from 28 January 1942. In fact, most of the first 20 Mustangs to arrive in Britain were initially used for evaluation and installation trials.

The AFDU at Duxford gave a very favourable report on the American fighter, praising in particular its handling. It noted that the cockpit, while generally spacious and comfortable, was a trifle cramped for a tall pilot. In addition it was excessively hot, even in freezing conditions. Compared to the Spitfire VB it was significantly faster at low and medium altitudes, but the speed advantage was lost at 25,000ft (7,600m). In rate of climb the Mustang was significantly inferior to the British fighter, by which it was outmanoeuvred at all heights. It did however perform far better in the dive as a result of its aerodynamic cleanness.

■ A MAJOR FLAW ■

The fall-off in performance with increasing altitude was the one flaw in an otherwise superb fighting aeroplane. From the first days of air fighting, altitude had always been regarded as the most important tactical advantage. By 1942, most air combat took place at altitudes where the Mustang was less agile. This being the case, RAF Fighter Command could not risk it, and the majority of the first batch of Mustang Is went to Army Co-operation Command squadrons, where their sparkling low-level performance and outstanding range could be fully utilized in the low-level armed reconnaissance role. For this they were fitted with an F24 oblique camera mounted behind the pilot's head armour.

Even as prophets are traditionally without honour in their own land, so the Mustang was for a long time ignored by the USAAF. Reasons were not hard to find; existing fighters such as the P-38 and P-40 were undergoing further development, while several new and promising designs were coming along fast, among them Republic's enormous P-47 Thunderbolt. Consequently there

Above: The seventh production Mustang I seen at the Air Fighting Development Unit, RAF Duxford, for which it had the yellow P in a circle painted on the fuselage. The carburettor scoop on this machine has been lengthened, and the adjustable outlet at the rear of the radiator farm can be seen open.
Right: The fourth and tenth production Mustangs were retained by the USAAC for evaluation under the designation XP-51. This was a departure from standard practice, as the X prefix was normally only given to true prototypes, which this was far from being. Seen here in RAF colours and apparently ready for delivery is AG 348, the fourth production machine, later renumbered as 41-038.

was little interest in what was primarily seen as a 'foreign' design. The USAAF did however acquire two examples of the type.

This had come about quite fortuitously. Before warplanes could be exported, the manufacturer needed a Foreign Release Agreement with the USAAC (as the USAAF then was). This agreement stated that the fourth and tenth production machines should be supplied for evaluation, with the designation XP-51. Although the first aircraft was flown on 20 May 1941, various delays ensured that it did not reach the test centre at Wright Field, Ohio (now Wright-Patterson AFB) until 24 August. The second XP-51 did not arrive until 16 December that year, by which time the official performance flight tests were all but complete.

The US government made credit available with lend lease

The first batch of Mustangs for the RAF was a straight sale, but with the costs of all-out war escalating, British funds ran short. At this stage the US government made credit available with Lend-Lease. Under this arrangement, the USAAF ordered aircraft as though for their own use, then passed them on. On 7 July 1941, the USAAF placed an order for 150 Mustangs on behalf of the RAF. These differed from the previous batch in that they were armed with four 20mm Hispano Suiza cannon in place of the previous eight machine guns, a change arising from extensive combat experience. In RAF service these became Mustang IAs; to the Americans they were plain P-51s, with no suffix letter.

With flight testing at Wright Field in full swing early in December 1941, the treacherous attack on Pearl Harbor by the Japanese catapulted the United States into the war. While this was to have a lasting effect on the future of the Mustang, at first it served only to obscure matters as American fighter development

Top: 41-038 seen at the Wright Field, Ohio, test centre (now Wright-Patterson AFB) some time after 24 August 1942. With the exception of an anti-dazzle panel on the cowling and bright national markings, the aircraft is in bare metal. Surprisingly, the carburettor scoop has not been lengthened, while the gun ports have either been blanked over, or airbrushed out by the censor. (USAF via JE)

Middle: 41-038 survived the war, albeit in a sad and careworn state. Seen here at Freeman Field in Indiana in 1945 and scheduled for the scrap yard, it was rescued for the National Air and Space Museum. (Haney Collection via JE)

Bottom: Completely refurbished by the Experimental Aircraft Association after 30 years in storage, 41-038 flew again in 1980 as part of the Warbirds of America fleet.

XP-51 OFFICIAL PERFORMANCE SUMMARY

Level Flight Speed at Design Altitude of 13,000ft (3,950m) with a Design Gross Weight of 7,934lb (3,600kg)

Maximum speed 382mph (615km/hr) 3,000 rpm/1,100bhp
High speed 370mph (595km/hr) 3,000rpm/1,100bhp
Cruising speed 325.5mph (524km/hr) 2,280rpm/750bhp

Optimum Range and Endurance with 170 imperial gallon fuel
Cruising speed 780 miles (1,255km) 2.4 hours

Climb Data with Gross Weight of 7,934lb(3,600kg)

Altitude	0/0	5,000/	10,000/	15,000/	20,000/	25,000/	30,800/
(ft/m)		1,524	3,0484	572	6,095	7,620	9,387
Climbing speed							
(mph/kh)	178/286	194/312	208/335	222/357	236/380	248/399	262/422
Engine (rpm)	3,000	3,000	3,000	2,600	2,600	2,600	2,600
Power (bhp)	1,050	1,095	1,140	820	680	550	–
Max climb							
ft/min	2,200	2,270	2,345	1,570	1,070	610	100
m/sec	11.18	11.53	11.91	7.98	5.44	3.10	0.51

and production was stepped up. The few Wright Field test pilots who had flown the Mustang were impressed, but they were lone voices crying in the wilderness. Only slowly were its sterling qualities recognized and accepted.

Of the 150 P-51s ordered for the RAF, only 93 were actually delivered to them. Of the remainder, 55 were retained by the USAAF, commencing in July 1942, by whom they were at first known as Apaches. Most of these were fitted with cameras to become F-6A tactical reconnaissance machines. The final two were earmarked for the XP-78 project, which involved a change of engine.

Massive expansion had caused budgetary problems for the USAAF, and by the time that it decided that it wanted the Mustang, the budget for fighters was exhausted. There was however still money in the kitty for an attack aircraft. Consultations between NAA and the Pentagon resulted in the A-36A Invader. In essence this was a P-51 with the uprated -87 Allison engine, underwing racks to carry two 500lb (227kg) bombs, and dive brakes. Hydraulically actuated, these were of the perforated door type, set above and below the wings. The 0.30in (7.62mm) machine guns in the wings were deleted.

■ DIVE-BOMBER PLOY ■

At this stage the USAAF had no requirement for a dive bomber, but modifying the P-51 in this way was a useful ploy for getting it into USAAF service. Be this as it may, this did not prevent the USAAF from evaluating the A-36A as a dive bomber. On 16 April 1942, a massive order for 500 A-36As was placed, long before this variant flew.

This was followed on 23 June (when the next year's budget became available) by another order for 310 P-51As. These used the latest model Allison V-1780-81 engine, which developed maximum power at 18,000ft (5,490m) and thus significantly improved high-altitude performance, although it still did not give the Mustang parity in this sphere with its European contemporaries. The other major change was in weaponry; the nose-mounted guns with their heavy and cumbersome synchronization gears, the latter necessary to prevent damage to the propeller, were deleted, as were the wing-mounted 0.30in (7.62mm) machine guns. The number of wing-mounted 0.50in (12.7mm) Browning heavy machine guns was increased to four.

This change in the armament offered

Left: **The angular lines of the Mustang made it easily mistaken for the rather smaller Me 109E. Seen here is the most heavily armed Mustang of all, the P-51 (no suffix letter), which carried four 20mm cannon in the wings. (Roger Freeman)**

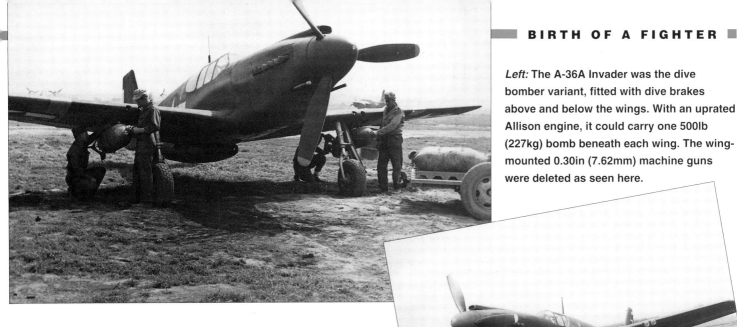

Left: The A-36A Invader was the dive bomber variant, fitted with dive brakes above and below the wings. With an uprated Allison engine, it could carry one 500lb (227kg) bomb beneath each wing. The wing-mounted 0.30in (7.62mm) machine guns were deleted as seen here.

several advantages. With the increasing use of armour plate and self-sealing tanks by the enemy, light machine guns had little to commend them, whereas the Browning .50s were adequate against all but heavy bombers, few of which were likely to be encountered. The projectile of the heavier gun had near-perfect ballistics (the world's first supersonic fighter, the Bell X-1, used the same shape for its fuselage) giving a long effective range. Weight saving was considerable. The complexity of the overlapping feeds for the wing guns was greatly reduced, while the logistical problems that arose from using two different sizes of ammunition were eliminated.

Right: P-51A of the USAAF. The wide spread of the main gear legs made it particularly suitable for operations from semi-prepared airstrips. (Roger Freeman)

USAAF reverted to the British name of Mustang

The A-36 made its maiden flight in the hands of test pilot Ben Chilton on 21 September 1942 – by which time the USAAF had reverted to using the British name of Mustang for all variants – and the same pilot also took the first P-51A into the air on 3 February 1943. With production by now in full swing,

Above: Reconnaissance Mustang! The F-6B was a P-51A fitted with a twin K24 camera installation. This 9th Air Force example is from the 107th Squadron of the 67th Tactical Reconnaissance Group. It is fitted with the Malcolm hood, a field modification invented by the British to improve all-round view from the cockpit. (T. R. Bennett via JE)

first deliveries of the latter took place during the following month. Of the 310 P-51As, 35 were fitted with the twin K24 camera installation to become F-6Bs, while 50 were allocated to the RAF as Mustang IIs.

The Mustang was by now well and truly launched in both RAF and USAAF service. But the best this fighter could produce was still to come.

FINAL REPORT

The A-36 has excellent diving characteristics from the standpoint of a fighter, but it dives too fast for a dive bomber, the dive breaks slowing the airplane down approximately eighty-three (83) miles per hour. This is insufficient from the dive bomber standpoint, as the airplane will still dive with the dive breaks open to speed in excess of four-hundred-fifty miles per hour, necessitating bomb release at approximately four thousand (4,000) feet in order to pull out of the dive. The best diving angle is approximately seventy (70) degrees.

EXTRACT FROM FINAL REPORT ON TEST OF THE OPERATIONAL SUITABILITY OF THE A-36 TYPE AIRPLANE, 15 APRIL 1943.

THE ROLLS-ROYCE ENGINE

The margin between success and failure is always slim. As fighters sought ever greater altitudes, the British need for the Allison-engined Mustang diminished. As it was, the type was rejected for the pure fighter role due to its poor high-altitude performance. Had the RAF not had a requirement for low-level tactical reconnaissance it might easily have been shunted off to some less important theatre of operations, there to languish largely unseen and unsung, until attrition removed it from the inventory.

On the other hand, the great wonder is that the Mustang was not designed with a more suitable engine from the start. Such an engine was available from the outset; the Rolls-Royce Merlin which powered the Spitfire and Hurricane, and a dozen other aircraft as well. As the Mustang was designed for the British, it is extremely surprising that such a power plant was not suggested at a very early stage. That the superb American airframe was eventually mated with the equally superb British engine appears to have been due as much to chance as anything. Be that as it may, it produced one of the truly great fighters of the Second World War, albeit rather belatedly.

■ SOMETHING BETTER ■

Late April 1942. The Mustang prototype had made its first flight almost exactly 18 months earlier, and AFDU was finalizing the test report on the production articles at Duxford. Meanwhile a new German fighter, the Focke-Wulf FW 190A, had entered large-scale service on the Channel coast. It comfortably outclassed the standard British fighter of the day, the Spitfire V. Almost overnight the RAF had slipped from a slight technical advantage to a position of undoubted inferiority. Something better was needed, urgently. This was the state of play when Rolls-Royce test pilot Ronald Harker visited Duxford.

Part of Harker's brief was to evaluate the performance of aircraft powered by engines built by companies other than Rolls-Royce. This included not only British competitors, but American

Opposite page: P-51B Mustangs of the 354th FG shepherd B-24 Liberators of the 458th Bomb Group over the sea. In proximity to the enemy, the American fighters would maintain a healthy distance from the guns of the bombers. (Roger Freeman)

Below: The Mustang X, a Rolls-Royce company conversion with a Merlin 65 engine. The intercooler radiator beneath the nose rather spoiled the sleek lines of the original aircraft. (Roger Freeman)

Left: NAA converted two Mustangs to take Packard-Merlin V-1650 engines as XP-78s, later redesignated XP-51Bs. The first to fly, 41-37352 seen here, was originally built as a P-51 for the RAF but was taken over by the USAAF when America entered the war. The 20mm cannon armament was retained. (USAF via JE)

Below: Drop tanks beneath the wings, a P-51B of 354th FG based at Boxted in Essex taxies out ready for takeoff. This variant carried only four guns. (Associated Press via Roger Freeman)

and captured German machines.

On this particular day, 30 April, Wing Commander Ian Campbell-Orde, commanding AFDU, invited Harker to try out the Mustang. A 30-minute flight impressed him tremendously, although he noted the fall-off of power at altitude. At the same time he realized that the new Merlin 61, with a two-stage supercharger, would make all the difference.

On his return to Rolls-Royce, he asked the chief engineer to calculate performance figures for such a machine. The results were startling. Maximum speed was 441mph (710km/hr). Not only was this 70mph (113km/hr) faster than the Allison Mustang, but it was achievable at 25,600ft (7,800m) – almost double the best altitude of the American fighter! If the calculations were correct, the combination was a potential world-beater. In some parameters it was better than the new Spitfire VIII powered by the same engine.

TEST FLYING

'Flying a new airplane I always put the power on easily at the start to get the feel of the airplane on the ground, then gradually gave it power. When I got airborne, a couple of hundred feet off the ground, I pulled up the gear and decided then I'd see how it would climb from scratch. I poured the coal to it and the aircraft snap-rolled! Rolls-Royce hadn't provided enough vertical fin area, and not enough offset.'

LT COL. CAS HOUGH, USAAF

■ TWO-STAGE MERLIN ■

The advent of the Merlin 61 was almost as fortuitous. By mid-1941, the engine had neared its development limits, and the future was thought to lie with the larger Griffon. There was however a requirement for a turbo-charged Merlin to power a high-altitude bomber. But turbo-superchargers, as American engine manufacturers knew well, were heavy, bulky, and complicated. As an alternative, Rolls-Royce hooked up two superchargers in series. The results were startling. Trial flights showed the full-throttle altitude as 29,750ft (9,070m); an amazing increase! Shortly after, the high-altitude bomber was cancelled and the new engine was developed for the Spitfire as the Merlin 61.

At first, interest in Harker's proposal was lukewarm, but as the new engine was expected to give the Spitfire little more than parity with the FW 190A, the prospect of a fighter which would clearly outperform the German machine was too tempting to resist. Five Mustang air-frames were acquired for trials.

The Americans had meanwhile been keeping a close watch on developments. Arrangements had been made for Packard to licence-build the Merlin as the V-1650 as long ago as October 1940. By 1942 American production of the British engine was in full flood, and arrangements for production of the Merlin 61 were well in hand. North American were fully in the picture, and also started planning a Mustang with the new engine.

■ HIGHER AND FASTER ■

Fortunately not too many modifications were needed. The Merlin was dimensionally similar to the Allison, although it was some 300lb (136kg) heavier. The extra weight was more than offset by about 600hp extra, plus the high-altitude capability that was so desperately needed. Rolls-Royce chose to design a new engine mount. The intercooler for the supercharger installation led to a small radiator under the nose, and this

Left: Fresh from the factory, this Block 1 P-51B shows off its beautifully clean lines, the low drag of which contributed materially to its superb performance.
Middle: Although seemingly a P-51B with USAAF insignia, this is actually a late-production Mustang III destined for the RAF (FX 883), and carries an RAF fin flash and RAF camouflage. The inboard kink of the wing leading edge is very apparent from this angle. (Paul Coggan via JE)
Bottom: A Texas-built P-51C. The only visible difference between this and a P-51B is in the radio mast at the rear of the cockpit. This is a late-production aircraft, completed at the time when bare aluminium was favoured over camouflage. While this was popularly supposed to increase maximum speed, differences between specific aircraft made it impossible to confirm. (Paul Coggan via JE)

location also housed the carburettor intake, giving a rather bulged effect to the front of the aeroplane and spoiling its clean lines.

The first flight of the Mustang X, as it was designated, took place at Hucknall on 13 October 1942. While all went well, it was quickly evident that the formerly pleasant handling qualities had been adversely affected by the changes. Torque from the more powerful engine and the four-bladed propeller reduced directional stability, particularly in the dive. To overcome this, a small dorsal spine was added to the rear fuselage just in front of the fin, to give extra keel area. Despite the draggy nose contours, the first Mustang X attained a level speed of 433mph (697km/hr), and reached 20,000ft (6,100m) in 6.3 minutes; barely two-thirds of the time taken by the Allison Mustang. But the P-51X was purely experimental, with Rolls-Royce feeding information back to NAA in California.

■ TWO-SEATER ■

Meanwhile NAA had also been moving fast. Authorization to convert two Mustangs to Merlins had been issued on 25 July. At first these were designated XP-78; only later did they become XP-51Bs. Whereas Rolls-Royce had spoiled the clean lines of the nose with

Above: A late-production P-51B, *Snoot's Sniper*, was given the Malcolm hood as a field modification. A sliding canopy, this could be opened in flight, unlike the previous 'lid and door' arrangement. This was an advantage on the landing approach in bad weather.

was easier said than done, and much redesign and intensive wind tunnel testing was needed to get it right.

Externally the P-51B differed little from the P-51A. The nose was slightly fatter, with the dorsal air scoop replaced by a less obvious ventral intake just behind the spinner. A Hamilton four-bladed propeller replaced the three-bladed one, and the radiator group under the mid-fuselage was slightly deeper. The structure had been beefed up internally, and hard points added beneath the wings to carry bombs. These were also plumbed for external drop tanks. Armament was standardized at four 0.50in (12.7mm) machine guns in the wings.

their conversions, with a consequent increase in drag and reduction in performance, NAA were extremely reluctant to do so. Urgent studies followed, which soon made it clear that the best location for the intercooler radiator was in with the group beneath the mid-fuselage. This

The first flight of the XP-51B took place on 30 November 1942, almost seven weeks later than the Rolls-Royce conversion, and immediately superior performance was evident. NAA test pilot Ben Chilton achieved a level speed of 441mph (710km/hr) at 29,800ft

Above: With a 75-gallon drop tank beneath each wing, the range of the P-51B was extended sufficiently to allow it to act as a long-range escort fighter. Its success in this role completely changed the bombing offensive against Germany.

Above right: This Mustang had a chequered career. Still crated, it was dropped in the sea while being unloaded, and badly damaged. Condemned to be reduced for spares, it was rebuilt as a two-seater, in which configuration it is seen here. It was finally lost in the Irish Sea in 1944 due to engine problems. (George Gosney via JE)

Right: P-51B of Don Blakeslee's 4th FG, seen late in 1944 after the switch from camouflage to natural metal finish. (Roger Freeman)

(9,080m), while the rate of climb against that of the P-51A was almost doubled. An order for 400 P-51Bs had been placed even before the prototype flew, and more large orders followed. Mass production was initiated, with a shadow factory at Fort Worth, Texas. Fort Worth Mustangs were virtually identical to those from Inglewood, but were designated P-51Cs.

The first production P-51B flew on 5 May 1943, and the first P-51C on 5 August of the same year. Photo-reconnaissance was still a requirement, and 71 P-51Bs and 20 P-51Cs were converted to carry two K24 oblique cameras, or a K17 and K22. In this guise they became F-6Cs, most of which retained their armament.

■ ESCORT FIGHTER ■

By mid-1943 the USAAF 8th Air Force was carrying the fight to Germany, but it was becoming increasingly evident that the heavy bombers were unable to protect themselves sufficiently. A long range escort fighter was needed. The P-47 Thunderbolt, although an excellent fighter in many ways, lacked range, while

Below: **Winter 1943–44. An early shipment of P-51Bs lined up at Speke airport, awaiting allocation to front-line units. (Roger Freeman)**

the twin-engined P-38 Lightning, though able to acquit itself well enough in theatres where the Allies held an overwhelming numerical advantage, was a turkey in the dogfight against the German single-engined single seaters.

The Fisher P-75A, an enormous, heavy, and complicated beast

Several large and expensive fighters were under development for the long-range escort role. Fairly typical of these was the Fisher P-75A, an enormous, heavy and complicated beast, which first flew in November 1943. Early trials were unpromising, and a requirement was issued for an extra fuel tank to be fitted in the fuselage of a P-51B. With two external drop tanks this increased the total fuel capacity of the Mustang to 348 imperial gallons (419 US gallons/1,586 litres). With this fuel load, the P-51B could do a round trip of over 1,200 miles (1,930km); rather more than the distance from England to Berlin and back.

Only the last few hundred P-51Bs and Cs were fitted with the fuselage tank as standard at the factory, although

P-51B/ MUSTANG III	
Dimensions	
Wingspan	37ft 0in (11.28m)
Length	32ft 3in (9.83m)
Height	13ft 8in (4.17m)
Wing area	233 sq. ft (21.65m²)
Weights	
Empty	7,000lb (3,175kg)
Normal TO	9,200lb (4,173kg)
Power	
Packard V-1650-7 inline rated at 1,720hp war emergency	
Performance	
Max. speed	422mph (711kph)
Climb	3,475fpm (18m/sec)
Range	950miles (1,529km)
Ceiling	42,500ft (12,953m)
Armament	
4 x 0.50in (12.7mm) machine guns	

some of the earlier production aircraft were retrofitted with it later. It did not feature on the Mustang III, as the P-51B was known in RAF and Commonwealth service.

There was of course a penalty to be paid. The extra weight so far back made directional stability rather marginal, and when half empty the petrol slopped about, affecting handling during what were quite mild manoeuvres. The drill was to take off, form up gently with the others, set course, then drone on steadily for the next hour or more, burning off fuel. Not until the fuselage tank was virtually empty could the pilot relax.

■ INTO SERVICE ■

Ordering a new aircraft type from the drawing board is unthinkable today, but during the war, things were different. A protracted development period, during which all the bugs were ironed out, simply meant that the in-service date might be delayed by a year, or even more. During this time, pilots would

Above: RAF Mustang IIIs in the Mediterranean theatre of operations retained the original canopy. This example is a P-51C of No. 260 Squadron, seen having a thorough overhaul in Termili, Italy. (Roger Freeman)

ROLL

'Upon returning from a mission with the right drop tank still attached, I flared out for landing with a 45 knot crosswind from 90° to the right. The airplane was trimmed heavily to the left, to hold up the right wing, due to the extra drag from the drop tank. As the airspeed decreased, just prior to touchdown, the tank dropped off. The right wing came up, and the wind started to roll the airplane to the left. I immediately applied full power. The torque, the wind, and the extreme left trim caused an immediate roll of 180°. I found myself inverted 50 feet off the ground and looking up through the canopy at pierced steel planking going by at 100 or so mph. I throttled back and sort of washed out in a half roll to the right.'

LT WILLIAM G. COLONEY USAAF,
5TH FS, 52ND FG, 15TH AF

have to make do with inferior or outdated machines, and all too often pay with their lives for the privilege. An underdeveloped but superior-performing machine rushed into service could also be a cause of fatalities, but its performance gave its pilot a better chance in the hazard of battle. It was a question of which omelette required the fewest broken eggs, and in general this was the latter course of action.

The first Merlin-Mustang unit to see action reached England in October 1943. The 8th Air Force had been eagerly awaiting the arrival of the new long-range fighter, but an administrative error saw it assigned to 9th Air Force for ground attack. A compromise resulted in it being made available for bomber escort with the 8th until such time as further P-51B Groups arrived. Not until the following spring was the type operational in quantity.

Technical problems were rapidly encountered. Engines running rough, propeller seal leaks spilling oil onto the

Right: P-51Ds of three fighter groups in Italy. Left to right, 332nd FG; 52nd FG, to which William G. Coloney was assigned; and 31st FG. (Roger Freeman)

Below: Closeup of the Malcolm hood, which was fitted to all British-based Mustang IIIs, and not a few Mustang IIs. Not only did it give far better all-round visibility, but it could be opened in flight. (Roger Freeman)

windshield, overheating for whatever reason, faulty engine mounting bolts. All were gradually cured. Sometimes the underwing drop tanks failed to feed; the solution was to pressurize them.

Far more serious was the problem of gun jamming. To fit the Brownings in the wings, they had to be canted at an angle, with the ammunition belts feeding over and down into the breeches. In a turn of more than 2g, the forces exerted exceeded the limits of the mechanism, and they jammed. In the middle of a dogfight this could be very embarrassing. Booster motors were fitted, but these were a long time arriving.

The 68 imperial gallon (85 US gallon/ 322 litre) fuselage tank not only led to directional instability in flight, it also caused such severe tail-heaviness that even take-off was an activity fraught with peril. Before long the load was restricted to 52 imperial gallons (65 US gallons/246 litres). A related problem was that a sudden pull on the stick caused a high-speed stall followed by a snap roll. This could however be put to good use by experienced pilots as an evasive manoeuvre that no enemy fighter was able to follow.

A procedure was initiated in which the fuel in the fuselage tank was used first, followed by that in the drop tanks. After a few instances in which Mustangs were

Below: **One Mustang IV ready for delivery to the RAF. This is actually a Texas-built P-51K. In all, 875 Mustang IVs entered service, two thirds of which were P-51Ks. (AAHS via JE)**

bounced by enemy fighters and forced to drop full wing tanks, this sequence was reversed.

Most serious of all was structural failure. Occasionally the wings came off a Mustang in a high-speed dive. There were two main causes for this. At very high speeds, the large doors of the ammunition bays began to bulge outwards. This distorted the wing to the stage where the stresses imposed were too great, and it parted company with the fuselage. The second cause was a tendency for the undercarriage to extend in flight, causing abnormal loads on the

Above: **F-6C Mustang of the 111th Tactical Reconnaissance Squadron, 12th Air Force, seen in southern France, late 1944. The oblique camera port can be seen in the lower rear fuselage. (Roger Freeman)**

wing. These faults were eventually cured, but too late for some pilots.

The P-51B entered RAF service as the Mustang III. However, at this late stage, it was decided that the cockpit canopy was 'totally unsuited to European conditions', something that could have been determined way back in

P-51/K, MUSTANG IV/IVA

Dimensions

Wingspan	37ft 0in (11.28m)
Length	32ft 3in (9.83m)
Height	13ft 8in (4.17m)
Wing area	235 sq.ft (21.83m²)

Weights

Empty	7,635lb (3,463kg)
Normal TO	10,100lb (4,581kg)

Power

Packard V-1650-7 incline rated
at 1,720hp war emergency

Performance

Max. speed	437mph (703kph)
Climb	3,475fpm (18m/sec)
Range	1,710miles (2,751km)
Ceiling	41,900ft (12,770m)

Armament

6 x 0.50in (12.7mm) machine guns

1940, before the first Mustang ever flew. In a series of field modifications, the Mustang III was fitted with a bulged sliding canopy similar to that of the Spitfire. This was the 'Malcolm Hood', which vastly improved the all-round view, especially rearwards. A few Mustang IIs were also modified in this way.

As previously noted, the P-51B/C had several operational shortcomings, and NAA commenced work to rectify these. With ever-greater importance being placed on the all-round view from the cockpit, NAA modified a P-51B to take a one-piece tear-drop sliding canopy, which involved cutting down the rear fuselage to accommodate it. First flown on 17 November 1943, the new canopy gave a first class view through 360 degrees. With other modifications, it formed the basis of the definitive Mustang, the P-51D, or P-51K when built at Fort Worth.

The next improvement made was to the armament. Four 0.50 guns were demonstrably inadequate, while the inability to fire in hard turns without them jamming was a serious handicap. Extensive redesign resulted in six 0.50s, all upright instead of canted, which virtually eliminated feed stoppages. The two inboard guns had 400 rounds each, while the other four each had 270 rounds.

The wing chord was increased at the root, making it slightly deeper and affecting the kink at the leading edge. The main gear was strengthened to take a much greater all-up weight, and the wheel bays were modified to suit.

The P-51D was supplied to the RAF as the Mustang IV

Directional stability with fuel in the fuselage tank was always marginal, and cutting down the fuselage made matters worse. To offset this, a small dorsal fin was added. The P-51D was supplied to the RAF as the Mustang IV, and the P-51K, which differed only in having a slightly different propeller, became the Mustang IVA in British service.

As was the case with all other Mustang variants, some were converted for photo-reconnaissance. Two cameras, a K17 and a K22, were fitted in the rear fuselage just ahead of the tailwheel. Camera ship designations were F-6D and F-6K, and so far as is known, all retained their armament.

■ AUSTRALIAN ■ MUSTANGS

Only a handful of Mustangs were built outside the USA. The Commonwealth Aircraft Corporation of Australia obtained a licence to build the P-51D in 1944, starting with the assembly of knocked-down kits supplied by NAA. These resulted in 80 CA-17 Mustang XXs, the first of which flew in April 1945, while indigenous production provided 40 CA-18 Mustang 21s; 14 Mustang 22s fitted with an F24 camera; and 66 Mustang 23s, which differed in having British-built Merlins. However, no Australian-built Mustangs became operational until after the war.

Below: **Many late P-51D/Ks had a small dorsal fin extension added to provide extra keel area and improve directional stability, which was always marginal with fuel in the fuselage tank. (Alvin Williams via JE)**

THE BOEING B-17
FLYING FORTRESS

PROLOGUE

Bremen, north-west Germany, 11 June 1943. 'We did not know that the lead plane of the group ahead of us had two of its engines blasted by flak and had slowed to a crawl over that landscape from which came bomb bursts and legions of Focke-Wulfs and Messerschmitts.

'Mo (Colonel Preston) was trying to avoid overrunning the bombers ahead of him. We were trying to avoid overrunning Mo, and so the group disintegrated . . . we had been taught that strict formation flying was as vital to us as the British square had once been to the infantry. Not for us the anarchic whooping attack en masse. To be uncovered from a formation's friendly fire was to be naked and next to dead.

'Seeing our ragged line zig-zagging on a bomb run, the enemy came at us like wolves after straggling sheep. We had moved in so close to Colonel Mo that our wing tip was almost within reach of his waist gunner. Bohn (the co-pilot) had never flown formation at high altitudes. Johnny (the pilot) was an experienced formation flyer, but he was sitting on an unexploded 20mm shell somewhere in his seat, and the thought paralysed him.

'Bohn's tactic was to follow Mo as a chick follows its mother. We were tucked in so tight that our spent shells bounced off the wings of a B-17 beneath us. We could see that in the low squadron there was not a single plane that did not have at least one feathered prop.

■ FLAK ■

'When we came to a wide bay we saw the German smoke pots cloaking our target, Wilhelmshaven. Out of the smoke rose a storm of flak, rocking *Tondelayo*, sending fragments through her metal skin, biting into her delicate electric nerves.

'I called out the heading for the target, but Bob was already on top of his sight. We could not bomb as a Group, but only in train, following the plane ahead, hoping to hit the submarine pens we could not see. The explosions billowed up above the veil of smoke, but we could not be sure of whether we were plastering the shipping, the bay, the harbour or the bistros, whorehouses, shops, and homes of Wilhelmshaveners.'

This was the first combat mission of Lieutenant Elmer Bendiner of the 527th Squadron of the 379th Bomb Group, based at Kimbolton, and a more frightening introduction to war could hardly be imagined. The cold at 25,000ft (7,600m) caused frost to form on the plexiglass windows of the bomber, obscuring the view and making enemy fighters hard to spot. Constant scraping was needed in order to keep them clear.

The Fortress's course had taken them over the German Bight, then a turn onto a southerly course towards Bremen, their primary target. Making landfall near Cuxhaven they encountered accurate flak, its shrapnel rattling against their aircraft. Still heading south, German fighters had come thundering in from the east with guns blazing, and the B-17 gunners fired back, filling their machine with cordite fumes. A nearby bomber caught fire and spiralled down.

Above: The 379th BG, one of whose early exploits is described here, returns to base at Kimbolton after a raid on Germany.

Above: The 379th BG lost 141 aircraft missing in action, but despite extensive flak damage to the nose this Fortress was not one of them. (USAF via Alfred Price)

■ ALTERNATE TARGET ■

Almost simultaneously *Tondelayo* was hit by a 20mm cannon shell from an FW190. It made a jagged hole beneath Bendiner's window, grazed his helmet, penetrated a bulkhead and then passed through one of the rudder pedals and the pilot's seat before finally lodging in his seat-type parachute.

As if this were not enough, Bremen was obscured by cloud and haze and the bombers turned west for Wilhelmshaven, their secondary target, where, as related, the bombing proved fairly haphazard. On return, Bendiner's B-17 was found to have sustained multiple hits but, with the exception of damage to the hydraulic braking system, most were superficial.

From an Air Force point of view the raid was moderately satisfactory. Of the 168 bombers that set out that morning, only eight failed to return. But as so often happened, the brunt of the losses had been borne by a single unit. Bendiner's 379th Bomb Group lost six aircraft on this one mission, and of that six, four were from the 527th Squadron.

Narrow escapes were the order of the day, not only for Bendiner and his pilot. Another B-17F from Kimbolton was hit in the cockpit and both pilot and copilot were seriously wounded. The aircraft was flown back and successfully landed by one of the gunners under instruction from the pilot. The standard tour of duty was 25 operational missions, but to the survivors of the 527th Squadron it seemed that they would not have to go this far.

Above: The right tailplane of this 91st BG was knocked off by a 'friendly' bomb over Bremen in June 1943. (USAF via Alfred Price)

Above: Bombs go down on the Focke-Wulf aircraft factory near Bremen. Attacks on German aircraft production were given priority at an early stage of the American daylight bombing campaign. (USAF via Alfred Price)

■ TACTICS ■

American bombers flew in close formation for mutual protection against fighters, thereby unfortunately providing a massed target for flak as well as sometimes engendering problems on the bombing run. When the lead aircraft of the leading Group lost two engines on the same side, it threw the following 379th Group into total disarray. As luck would have it, the German fighters arrived on the scene, just when the formation was at its most vulnerable, and this, more than anything else, accounts for the heavy losses sustained by this unit. Throughout the war, formations and tactics were continually modified to find the best solutions to these problems.

As the war progressed, Fortresses ranged the length and breadth of Europe, the Mediterranean and North Africa, not to mention the Pacific theatre. Their first operational bombing sorties were made by the Royal Air Force even before the USA entered the war, and the type served with the British throughout, mainly with Coastal Command on anti-U-boat patrols over the Atlantic. Others flew over Germany at night in the electronic warfare role.

■ PACIFIC/FAR EAST ■

In American service they were present on Hawaii and the Philippines when Japan attacked Pearl Harbor, and were later seen in the skies of India, Java, New Guinea and Australia. Fortresses played a

Above: A German fighter pounces on a straggler from the 100th BG. (USAF via Alfred Price)

Above: While nose art was frequently of the 'girlie' type, it depended more on the predilections of the aircraft captain. The pilot of *Hard Seventeen* appears to have been a gamblin' man! (Ralph Trout)

peripheral role in the decisive naval Battle of Midway in June 1942, but were largely supplanted by B-24 Liberators in the Pacific Theatre of Operations from September 1943. But it is the strategic bombing of Germany for which they are best remembered, penetrating to the farthest corners of the Third Reich. Even when casualties were at their highest, the Fortress raids never turned back. The operational swan song of the Fortress came long after the war, when Israel used it against Egypt.

The practice of naming individual aircraft was almost universal in the United States Army Air Force, and was usually illustrated by graphic nose art. For example, *Tondelayo* was a character portrayed by Hedy Lamarr in a Hollywood film called *White Cargo*, depicted on the aircraft in a state of semi-undress. But not all the inspiration came from the cinema. Some aircraft bore warlike names, while others were references to crewmen or home towns. The most famous of all was of course *Memphis Belle*, the first B-17 to complete a full tour of 25 operational missions before returning to the USA in triumph to help sell war bonds.

Naming endowed a machine with a personality and carried with it the tacit belief that she – never it, always she – would bring her crew safely through. The aeroplane thus became a lucky charm, an amulet belonging to the entire crew, within which they were protected. When the aircraft's luck ran out, as it so often did, the crew went with it. But if, as happened from time to time, a Fortress brought its crew back but was so badly damaged that it had to be scrapped, it was sometimes the case that the replacement aircraft was given the same name with the suffix II added, thus transferring the luck from the old to the new.

1 Rudder construction
2 rudder tab
3 Rudder tab actuation
4 Tail gunner's station
5 Gunsight
6 Twin .50in (12.7mm) machine-guns
7 Tail cone
8 Tail gunner's seat
9 Ammunition troughs
10 Elevator trim tab
11 Starboard elevator
12 Tailplane structure
13 Tailplane front spar
14 Tailplane/fuselage attachment
15 Control cables
16 Elevator control mechanism
17 Rudder control linkage
18 Rudder post
19 Rudder centre hinge
20 Fin structure
21 Rudder upper hinge
22 Fin skinning
23 Aerial attachment
24 Aerials
25 Fin leading-edge de-icing boot
26 Port elevator
27 Port tailplane
28 Tailplane leading-edge de-icing boot
29 Dorsal fin structure
30 Fuselage frame
31 Tailwheel actuation
32 Toilet
33 Tailwheel (retracted) fairing
34 Fully-swivelling retractable tailwheel
35 Crew entry door
36 Control cables
37 Starboard waist hatch
38 Starboard waist .50in (12.7mm) machine gun
39 Gun support frame
40 Ammunition box
41 Ventral aerial
42 Waist gunners' positions
43 Port waist .50in (12.7mm) machine gun
44 Ceiling control cable runs
45 Dorsal aerial mast
46 Ball turret stanchion support
47 Ball turret stanchion
48 Ball turret actuation mechanism
49 Support frame
50 Ball turret roof
51 Twin .50in (12.7mm) machine guns
52 Ventral ball turret
53 Wingroot fillet
54 Bulkhead
55 Radio operator's compartment
56 Camera access hatch
57 Radio compartment windows (port and starboard)
58 Ammunition boxes
59 Single .30in (7.62mm) dorsal machine gun
60 Radio compartment roof glazing
61 Radio compartment/ bomb bay bulkhead
62 Fire extinguisher
63 Radio operator's station (port side)
64 Handrail links
65 Bulkhead step
66 Wing rear spar/ fuselage attachment
67 Wingroot profile
68 Bomb-bay central catwalk
69 Vertical bomb stowage racks (starboard installation shown)
70 Horizontal bomb stowage (port side shown)
71 Dinghy stowage
72 Twin .50in (12.7mm) machine guns
73 Dorsal turret
74 Port wing flaps
75 Cooling air slots
76 Aileron tab (port only)
77 Port aileron
78 Port navigation light
79 Wing skinning
80 Wing leading edge de-icing boot
81 Port landing light
82 Wing corrugated inner skin
83 Port out wing fuel tank (nine inter-rib cells)
84 No. 1 engine nacelle

BOEING B-17 FLYING FORTRESS

115 Flight deck underfloor control linkage
116 Wingroot/fuselage fairing
117 Wing front spar/ fuselage attachment
118 Battery access panels (wingroot leading-edge)
119 No. 3 engine nacelle spar bulkhead
120 Intercooler pressure duct
121 Mainwheel well
122 Oil tank (nacelle inboard wall)
123 Nacelle structure
124 Exhaust
125 Retracted mainwheel (semi-recessed)
126 Firewall
127 Cooling gills
128 Exhaust collector ring assembly
129 Three-blade propellers
130 Undercarriage retraction struts
131 Starboard mainwheel
132 Axle
133 Mainwheel oleo leg
134 Propeller reduction gear casing
135 1,000hp Wright R-1829-65 radial engine
136 Exhaust collector ring
137 Engine upper bearers
138 Firewall
139 Engine lower bearers
140 Intercooler assembly
141 Oil tank (nacelle outboard wall)
142 Supercharger
143 Intake
144 Supercharger waste-gate
145 Starboard landing light
146 Supercharger intake
147 Intercooler intake
148 Ducting
149 No. 4 engine nacelle spar bulkhead
150 Oil radiator intake
151 Main spar web structure
152 Mid-wing fuel tank rib cut-outs
153 Auxiliary mid spar
154 Rear spar
155 Landing flap profile
156 Cooling air slots
157 Starboard outer wing fuel tank (nine inter-rib cells)
158 Flap structure
159 Starboard aileron
160 Outboard wing ribs
161 Spar assembly
162 Wing leading-edge de-icing boot
163 Aileron control linkage
164 Wing corrugated inner skin
165 Wingtip structure
166 Starboard navigation light

85 Cooling gills
86 Three-blade propellers
87 No. 2 engine nacelle
88 Wing leading-edge de-icing boot
89 Port mid-wing (self-sealing) fuel tanks
90 Flight deck upper glazing
91 Flight deck/bomb-bay bulkhead
92 Oxygen cylinders
93 Co-pilot's seat
94 Co-pilot's control column
95 Headrest/armour

96 Compass installation
97 Pilot's seat
98 Windscreen
99 Central control console pedestal
100 Side windows
101 Navigation equipment
102 Navigator's compartment upper window (subsequently replaced by ceiling astrodome)
103 Navigator's table
104 Side gun mounting
105 Enlarged cheek windows (flush)

106 Ammunition box
107 Bombardier's panel
108 Norden bombsight installation
109 Plexiglass frameless nose-cone
110 Single .50in (12.7mm) machine gun
111 Optically-flat bomb-aiming panel
112 Pitot head fairing (port and starboard)
113 D/F loop bullet fairing
114 Port mainwheel

INTO BATTLE

By an irony of fate, the Flying Fortress did not make its combat debut in either its designed role of coastal defence, or even in the service of its country of origin. Instead it went to war as a high-altitude bomber with the Royal Air Force.

Even with the British, the Fortress got off to an unpromising start. With war looming, a British Purchasing Commission visited the United States in 1938 to investigate the possibility of acquiring American aircraft. With it was a certain Air Commodore Arthur Harris, later to become famous as Commander-in-Chief of RAF Bomber Command between 1942 and 1945. Among other types, he inspected a Y1B-17 of the 2nd Bombardment Group at Langley Field. Never a man for mincing words, Harris was scathing on the subject of its gun armament, and concluded that it was far

Left: As the Japanese swept across the Pacific, the Panama Canal took on a new importance. B-17s spent many weary hours patrolling the area. This is a B-17E with the early ventral turret. (USAF)

Below: A Messerschmitt Me 109 can just be seen in front of B-17F *Virgin's Delight* of the 91st BG, performing the Split-S breakaway manoeuvre. (USAF)

too vulnerable against any modern fighter. His comment on the nose cupola was that it was 'more appropriately located in an amusement park than in a war aeroplane'.

At the time, this was of course fair comment. But as we saw in the preceding chapter, Boeing and the USAAC were aware of these and other shortcomings, and were making every effort to correct them. By the end of 1940, the single most glaring deficiency was the lack of a power-operated gun turret.

By this time, the RAF had discovered

Above: Boeing got the serial letters wrong on the batch of Fortress Is for the RAF; they should be AN, not AM. On the left is Air Chief Marshal Sir Hugh Dowding, the former head of RAF Fighter Command during the Battle of Britain. (Bruce Robertson)

through hard and bloody experience that daylight raids on targets in the Third Reich, where strong fighter opposition might be encountered, were likely to incur unacceptable losses. There did, however, seem to be one possible solution to this.

ME 109E

The Messerschmitt Me 109E was the standard German interceptor during 1940 and most of 1941, and thus was the fighter that the Fortress I had to defeat. Powered by a Daimler-Benz 601 liquid-cooled engine, it could achieve a maximum speed of 354mph (570km/hr) at 12,500ft (3,800m). While its service ceiling was marginally better than that of the Fortress I, speed, rate of climb and manoeuvrability were all greatly reduced at extreme altitudes.

Above: Belly landing! A B-17 of the 379th BG touches down tail-first at Kimbolton. The ball turret has been jettisoned and all looks good. This group flew more sorties and dropped a greater weight of bombs than any other. (Bill Smith)

The standard German day fighter of the period was the Messerschmitt Me 109E. Leaving aside the brochure figures quoted for rate of climb and time to altitude of this aircraft, and instead allowing for a standing start scramble, time to join up, and a formation battle climb, which was always slower than could be accomplished by a single machine, it would take something over 30 minutes for the fighters to reach 30,000ft (9,150m). And once they did get there, both their maximum speed and their manoeuvrability would be greatly reduced.

■ WAS HEIGHT ■ THE KEY?

In the space of 30 minutes, a bomber cruising at 180mph (290km/hr) would cover a distance of 90 miles (145km). At that time there was little information about the German early warning system, but unless this could provide significantly more than half an hour's notice of impending attack, the chances were that the bombers would be able to do their work and be long gone before the fighters arrived. And even if adequate early warning was available, ground control would need to be very precise in order to position the fighters correctly for an interception.

Flying at such extreme altitudes appeared to offer bombers relative immunity from fighter interception, and almost total immunity from flak. A trio of British four-engined heavy bombers was entering service at about this time, but they were unable to reach such a high perch. Only the Flying Fortress had sufficient altitude capability, and of course this was coupled with the much-vaunted accuracy of the the top-secret Norden bombsight.

■ TRIALS AND ■ TRIBULATIONS

Initial British approaches for the Fortress were made in the summer of 1940, but not until the end of the year was the request approved, when 20 B-17Cs were released. Unfortunately these were not fitted with self-sealing fuel tanks, and had to be returned to Boeing for these to be installed. The delay thus caused was considerable, and not until April 1941 were the first four aircraft ready for delivery.

The first B-17C, known in RAF service as the Fortress I, arrived at Watton in Norfolk on 14 April. Others followed, and by the end of the third week in May, 14 had been delivered. Certain modifications were needed; standard British radio and signals equipment, identification lights etc., and all guns except the one in the nose were replaced by .50 Brownings. Most important of all

FORTRESS 1

Fortress I of No. 90 Squadron, RAF Bomber Command, the specially formed unit which pioneered very high altitude bombing, and with which the Flying Fortress made its combat debut. This aircraft, AN 530, *F for Freddie*, had an eventful career. It arrived in England on 10 July 1941; just too late to take part in the initial raid on Wilhelmshaven but, as one of the more reliable aircraft, it was selected for the abortive Berlin raid on 23 July. On 2 August it fought off attacks by three Me 109Fs of 3/JG 52, shooting down Feldwebel Wilhelm Summerer and damaging the other two. It was later transferred to No. 220 Squadron of Coastal Command and struck off charge in September 1943. (Bruce Robertson)

was the bombsight. The Norden was still top secret and had not been released; however RAF Fortresses were to have the Sperry Mk 0-1, similarly precise but rather more complex. This was duly installed, together with a Sperry auto-pilot system which, coupled to the sight, allowed the bomb aimer to make flat turns while lining up on target.

The recipient of the Fortress I was No. 90 Squadron, which was faced with the initial task of selecting men physically capable of standing up to the extremely demanding high-altitude operational environment. This was far from easy; nearly two-thirds of applicants failed for medical reasons. This made progress in forming the squadron slow.

As soon as sufficient personnel had been accepted and crewmen had been converted onto type (with the aid of a few selected American flyers and ground crew), high-altitude training was initiated. This revealed a number of problems.

The USAAC considered the optimum bombing altitude to be 20,000ft (6,100m), whereas the RAF proposed operating the Fortress I at least 50 per cent higher, and probably even more, in temperatures of –40° Celsius or even lower.

■ PROBLEMS ■

Two related factors caused unexpected problems; the first was the extremely low temperature and atmospheric pressure encountered at 30,000ft (9,150m) and above; the second was the delta temperature and atmospheric pressure; the difference between ground level and high altitude. These played havoc with the engines and other systems.

The former caused many Cyclones (but not all) to throw oil from the crankcase breather pipes. The turbo-superchargers became unduly sensitive to hamfisted control movements, surging at the least provocation, with the turbine blower breaking up in consequence. Heated window panels were needed to keep them clear of frost, while the auto-pilot/bombsight coupling caused violent yaws if the gyros had not been synchronized beforehand. The extreme changes in temperature and pressure during the course of a standard mission caused engine exhaust flanges to fracture, and

was responsible for hydraulic leaks which allowed air to infiltrate the system; a circumstance that was hardly conducive to effective braking.

Watton was a grass field not really suitable for such heavy machines, and pending the completion of a new airfield at Polebrook, with hard runways and taxiways, No. 90 Squadron moved to Great Massingham. It was during a flight from here, shortly before the projected move to Polebrook, that the first serious accident occurred.

The first USAAF casualty on active service occurs

It was June, the month in which the US Army Air Corps became the US Army Air Force. A Fortress I on a training flight over Yorkshire failed to climb above a thunderhead, and instead entered it. Once inside, the giant bomber was pounded by huge hailstones, while a thick layer of ice built up on the wings. This destroyed the lift, forcing the huge bomber into a death-dive. As it tumbled from the sky, the forces exerted on the unlucky machine wrenched off a wing then tore the fuselage in half. The only

Above: **The 305th BG which, under the command of Curtis LeMay, did so much to get the tactics right. Station-keeping in the formation ahead appears to leave much to be desired. (USAF via Alfred Price)**

survivor was Flight Lieutenant Steward, a medical officer from the Royal Aircraft Establishment at Farnborough, who managed to parachute to safety. Among the dead was Lieutenant Bradley, an experienced American B-17 pilot. He was the first airman of the newly constituted USAAF to die on active service.

■ FIRST ACTION ■

The essentials for a very high altitude bombing mission were two-fold; clear weather and near-perfect visibility. However good the aircraft and its crew, and however accurate the bombsight may be, if the target area cannot be identified from many miles away, and what is more the actual target cannot be clearly seen from nearly 6 miles (9km) up, there is little point in even starting out. These conditions were met on 8 July, and three Fortresses were duly despatched from Polebrook. The crews, led by the squadron commander, Wing Commander MacDougall, were perhaps not as well trained as they might have been, but political pressure was exerted

Above: Damaged over Bremen, this 100th BG Fortress made a spectacular crash-landing when a propeller came off after touch-down. Over 800 holes were counted from the radio room aft. (John Kidd)

by those eager to see how the big bird would acquit itself in action.

The target was Wilhelmshaven. The three Fortress Is were to fly there in loose formation, closing up only if fighters were encountered. They would bomb the naval base individually from 30,000ft (9,150m) with four American-type 1,100lb (500kg) bombs, then, divested of their loads and homeward bound, climb away from the target area to make the task of interception even more difficult.

As Robbie Burns once observed, 'The best laid plans of mice and men gang oft agley!' He might have added aviators. On the climb-out from base, all four engines of one Fortress started throwing oil, which streamed back and froze on the tail surfaces. This set up intense vibration, forcing its pilot to abandon the main mission and seek a target of opportunity.

The other two pressed on. They reached Wilhelmshaven and attacked with no intervention from the defences, but two bombs on the leading aircraft failed to release due to a frozen solenoid. This was the first of many failures caused by a combination of extreme cold and high humidity. On trials the Americans had not gone so high, nor was there

much humidity over the bombing ranges in Nevada or Utah. Humidity in particular bedevilled Fortress operations for the next two years. But even the bombs that did drop missed their targets. It was later concluded that the physical problems encountered at high altitude in unpressurized aircraft were greater than had been thought, and made bombing accuracy very hard to achieve. All in all, it was hardly to be regarded an auspicious combat debut.

After the Fortresses left the target area, two black specks were sighted climbing towards them by Tom Danby, a beam gunner in the squadron commander's aircraft. Fighters! The Fortresses lifted their noses and climbed labori-

ously, but to no avail. The Messerschmitt Me 109s easily drew level with Danby's aircraft, passed across the nose as if taking the measure of this enormous stranger, then one started to turn in astern. Danby lined up his sight and took first pressure on the trigger. As he did so, his pilot commenced a gentle turn towards the direction of attack. This forced the German pilot to tighten his turn, but as he did so, his wings lost their grip on the rarified air and he literally fell out of the sky! No shooting was done by either side, which was probably just as well because there was more than a fair chance that the guns of the Fortress were frozen up.

The next raid was a complete fiasco. On 23 July, three Fortresses set out to attack Berlin in daylight. Over Denmark they started leaving long white contrails, pointers in the sky that led the fighters straight to them. Far below, the crewmen could see menacing black specks, frantically grabbing for height but as yet nowhere near them. Over Denmark, the three Fortresses turned southwards towards Berlin, only to be faced with a solid wall of cloud. With no chance of locating their targets through it, they turned back, frozen and frustrated.

Below: Pillars of dark smoke denote hits on an oil refinery by the preceding wave, as more bombers bore in to attack. (USAF via Alfred Price)

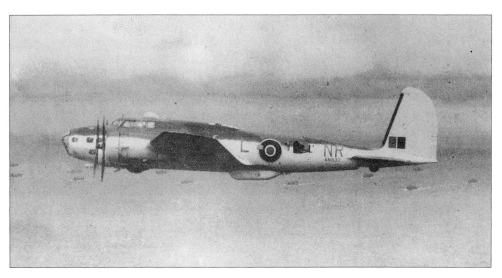

Above: Fortress I, formerly of No. 90 Squadron, seen here in the colours of No. 220 Squadron Coastal Command, escorting a convoy across the Atlantic. (Alfred Price)

Other raids followed. On 24 July Brest was attacked, and hits were claimed on the battle cruisers *Scharnhorst* and *Gneisenau*. Emden was raided two days later. So far the German fighters had failed to intercept, but this situation did not last. On 2 August a Fortress was attacked north of Texel at only 22,000ft (6,700m) by three Me 109Fs, which made seven passes at the bomber, hitting it, but fortunately not seriously. Remarkably, one German fighter was shot down into the sea, a second was damaged and force-landed, while the third suffered some minor damage from the Fortress's return fire.

The first high-altitude fighter engagement that took place was a much more

Below: Nineteen B-17Fs served with RAF Coastal Command as the Fortress II. This aircraft was written off in the Azores in 1944 after a taxiing accident. (Bruce Robertson).

deadly affair. The same crew was caught at 32,000ft (9,750m) over Brest by seven Messerschmitts on 16 August and subjected to 26 attacks in quick succession.

Even at high altitude the B-17 proved vulnerable to fighters

The pilot put the big bomber into a shallow dive for maximum speed, taking evasive action against each attack. Eventually he escaped into cloud, but not before two crewmen had been killed and another two wounded. The Fortress crashed on landing and burned. Then a four-aircraft attack against the German pocket battleship *Admiral Scheer* at Oslo on 8 September also encountered fighters. One bomber was shot down, another went missing without trace. The third returned too badly damaged to be repairable. The writing was on the wall.

Even at high altitude the Fortress I was proving too vulnerable in daylight, the bomb load was too small and the bombing too inaccurate.

The final Fortress operational mission from Polebrook was flown on 25 September, bringing the total to 48 sorties, 26 of which were aborted for various reasons, the most frequent of which was cloud obscuring the target. At this point, four aircraft were detached to Egypt, from where they carried out maritime reconnaisance missions over the Mediterranean, and night attacks on Tobruk and other North African targets. It was however found that the heat and dust of the desert reduced performance and serviceability quite spectacularly, and the two survivors of this period were sent to India, where they were eventually handed over to the USAAF.

Back at Polebrook, experimental high-altitude flights continued for a while. By this time the oil throwing and freezing-up of the guns had largely been cured, and the main purpose was to investigate the physiological problems more fully. This finally came to an end, and the remaining Fortress Is were transferred to No. 220 Squadron of Coastal Command, with whom they ranged far out over the Atlantic on anti-submarine patrols.

■ PACIFIC CRUCIBLE ■

By December 1941, the USAAF was in possession of about 150 Flying Fortresses. Mainly these were based in the continental USA, but some flew anti-submarine patrols from Newfoundland. These were reconnaissance missions only, because America was still officially neutral. Yet other Flying Fortresses were deployed in the Pacific.

Above: Action replay of the Pearl Harbor attack, as a 'Japanese Zero' swoops down on a landing Fortress at the annual air show at Oshkosh. The B-17 is specially modified to put one main gear and the tail wheel down to simulate battle damage. (Eric Lundahl)

Below: Conditions in the Pacific could be primitive. This aircraft made a wheels-down forced landing on a Papua New Guinea beach. After repair, the locals were enlisted to help lay a steel matting runway to allow it to take off. (Both Frank F. Smith)

The 19th Bombardment Group was based at Hickam Field, right next door to Pearl Harbour on Oahu in the Hawaiian Islands. In the Philippines, at that time an American Protectorate, were 35 B-17Cs and Ds of the 7th Bombardment Group, based at Clark Field. Both Groups were about to be reinforced, and a dozen aircraft were in transit to them. This was the situation when Japanese carrier aircraft made a surprise strike against the American fleet at Pearl Harbour on the 7th of the month, an attack which finally brought America into the war.

At Hickam Field, the 19th Bombardment Group was caught on the ground by the Japanese attack, and all 12 aircraft were destroyed. Worse was to follow. The reinforcements for the 7th and 19th Bombardment Groups arrived at the height of the raid; low on fuel and unarmed, they were unable to defend themselves. Four were destroyed and all the others damaged, some by Japanese fighters, others by 'friendly' ground fire.

Just hours later, the Japanese turned their attention to the Philippines, destroying 14 B-17s of the 19th Bombardment Group on the ground at Clark Field. It was fortunate that a single squadron from this group had been deployed to Del Monte on Mindanao, 200 miles (320km) further south, so some of the group escaped this attack unscathed.

The surviving Fortresses of the 19th were employed against the Japanese invasion force, with little success, for ships at sea proved elusive targets. Hits were often claimed, but in fact little damage was done.

Fighter opposition at this time was provided by the redoubtable Mitsubishi A6M2 Zero, and two notable encounters with Fortresses took place in the first few days of fighting. On 10 December, a Japanese landing force consisting of one light cruiser, six destroyers and four transports, was off-loading at Vigan on Luzon. At an altitude of 18,000ft (5,500m) above them flew 27 covering Zeros, one of them piloted by Saburo Sakai, later to become the top surviving Japanese fighter ace (62 kills).

Six B-17Ds of the 14th Bombardment Squadron were sent against the invaders. They bombed from 25,000ft (7,600m), and succeeded in doing little damage. One of their number, piloted by Lieutenant Colin Kelly Jr, was spotted after the attack, and seven avenging Zeros set off in hot pursuit.

The Zeros were slower than their European counterparts, and in any case had additional height to gain. Not until 100 miles (160km) further on did they catch the speeding bomber. Even before they could gain a firing position, three other Zeros appeared ahead and attacked from above, but with absolutely no effect.

At last the pursuers caught up, and joined with the other three in line astern, making pass after pass, again with no apparent effect. The chase lasted a further 50 miles (80km), taking them over the US base at Clark Field. Sakai then took a hand. With two other fighters in attendance he closed right in, braving

ZERO FIGHTER

The Mitsubishi Zero was optimized for dogfighting rather than bomber interception. Japanese engines of the time lacked power, and to maximize manoeuvrability and performance by reducing weight, the Zero had no armour plating, no self-sealing fuel tanks, and often no radio. It was therefore very vulnerable to return fire.

Above: **Some had it easier than others. General MacArthur's personal transport, *Bataan*, had reclining seats and hot and cold running water installed. (USAF)**

Below: **Declared 'war-weary' on the arrival of the B-17F, this E-model became a personal transport for General George Kenney. (USAF)**

against a Fortress, which was an extremely tough aircraft indeed. Wheless' B-17D sustained over 1,000 hits and still kept flying, although it was eventually wrecked in the ensuing forced landing on Mindanao.

■ THE B-17 ■ ENTERS SERVICE

The Japanese overran the Philippines by the end of December, and the handful of Fortresses were pulled back to Darwin in Northern Australia. From here it was about 1,500 miles (2,400km) to targets in the southern Philippines, which meant that even with auxiliary fuel tanks in the bomb bay, the bomb load that could be carried was exceedingly small; less than two tons in many cases. Shortly after, the B-17s were sent to Java. There were so few of them, but they were the only aircraft available with the necessary range to reach Japanese bridgeheads in Borneo and elsewhere, and even then they needed to stage through those Allied airfields which had not yet fallen.

By now the improved B-17E was entering service, and more than 50 of these were sent to reinforce the theatre, although due to Japanese successes they were forced to come the long way round, via Africa and India. Attrition was heavy; nearly two-thirds of the available Fortresses were lost in the first three months of the Pacific War, to accidents as well as enemy action. During this period, Fortresses claimed to have sunk three warships, including the battleship *Haruna*, and eight transports, in the course of some 350 sorties. One bombardier actually claimed hits on ships when bombing from 35,000ft (10,700m) which says as much for his optimism as his eyesight. In fact, Japanese records showed that only two transports probably succumbed to air attack by Fortresses.

After two months operating out of airfields on Java the Allies had to evacuate in the face of Japanese advances, and once more the surviving Fortresses found themselves back in Australia. But by this time, very few of the original B-17Cs and Ds were left, and their replacement, the B-17E, was a very different bird indeed.

the defensive fire. Fuel streamed back from the ruptured tanks of the bomber, its gunners ceased firing, and fire broke out in the fuselage. It was the end. His crew baled out, but Kelly himself did not manage to escape. It was the first Flying Fortress to fall to Japanese fighters in the Pacific.

Four days later, a battle against even heavier odds ended differently. On 14 December, a B-17D of the 19th Bombardment Group piloted by Lieutenant Hewitt Wheless became separated from its formation. When he was just about to bomb a Japanese freighter from low altitude, he found himself bounced by 18 Zeros.

The Japanese fighters made attack after attack on the lone bomber, knocking out the left outboard motor, the radio and the oxygen system, shooting off the tail wheel, riddling the fuselage, holing the fuel tanks, damaging the control runs and killing one crewman. The Fortress gunners fought back desperately, claiming three fighters shot down, but their guns either jammed or ran out of ammunition. It looked like the end of the road, but fortunately the remaining Japanese fighters had also run out of ammunition.

This was perhaps less surprising than it may seem. Zeros carried a mere five seconds-worth of ammunition for their 20mm cannon, while their rifle-calibre machine guns were virtually useless

When in December 1941 the USA entered the war, both the RAF and the USAAF were agreed on one thing: for the immediate future, the Third Reich could only be effectively attacked from the air. The primary disagreement was as to how. As a result of hard and bloody experience, the RAF had, with a few notable exceptions, abandoned daylight raids in favour of the cover of darkness, and argued strongly that the Americans should join them in this.

The USAAF, however, was not convinced. The British night effort at this time was fairly agricultural, with many crews unable to land their bombs within 5 miles (8km) of their targets. It consisted of little more than exporting bombs to 'somewhere in Germany'. Area bombing, which was to devastate German cities in the next three years, had not yet matured. The truth was that while night attacks tied down valuable

Left: Fortresses of the 381st BG leave contrails emblazoned across the sky, while two fighters hurtle across them high above. (USAF)
Below: Typical European weather made navigation, target finding and accurate bombing far more difficult than the USAAF expected. B-17F *Meat Hound* of the 306th BG in cloudy skies. (USAF)

Above: 8th AF commander General Jimmy Doolittle talks to a weather reconnaissance crew on their return. Second from left is Flying Officer Eldridge, an RAF weather observer. (USAF)

German resources in the shape of flak and night fighters, they were at that time doing little real damage.

The USAAF view was that precision attacks on industrial targets would be far more effective, and these could only be carried out in daylight. Daylight made accurate navigation much easier, and also the precise identification of industrial complexes. The American Norden

massed firepower of their defensive armament to beat off the German fighters. The new and better protected B-17E and F were coming on stream, and the vulnerability against attack from astern had been reduced. The British prophesied disaster, but the Americans were confident in adopting the 'wagon train' approach of their forebears.

But before operations could start, there was much to be done. RAF Bomber Command was expanding fast, and new airfields sprang up like mushrooms across England. Even more airfields were needed for their American allies, and providing these took time.

■ THE FIRST ■ BOMB GROUP

Nor was the USAAF ready initially. The basic unit was the Bombardment Group (BG), which consisted of a headquarters and three squadrons, quickly increased to four, each of which had an establishment of 8–10 aircraft. The demand for personnel, training and aircraft initially outstripped supply. Matters were not helped when many production Fortresses were sent to units in the Pacific. It was months before the first USAAF Bombardment Group (Heavy) was able to take off and point its Fortresses eastwards, across the cold grey Atlantic.

Above: **Airfields for the USAAF bombers were hastily prepared. An open-air bomb dump at Framlingham, with tented accommodation. (USAF).**
Left: **'Fill 'er up and check the oil, please!' For a raid on Germany, 2,000 gallons of fuel per aircraft was not exceptional. (USAF).**

tachometric bomb sight was inherently far more accurate than the British Mk XIV vector sight. On the bombing range in peacetime in clear visibility, releasing from an altitude of 10,000ft (3,050m), circular error probability (the radius within which the best 50 per cent of bombs fall) was about 300ft (90m) for the Norden and 775ft (235m) for the Mk XIV.

In combat, things were less simple. Heavy and accurate flak forced the bombers to much greater altitudes. Not only did circular error probability increase significantly with height, but shrapnel rattling against the wings and fuselage was a considerable distraction to the bombardier. European weather conditions bore no similarity to those of California, and frequently the target was obscured or semi-obscured by cloud. All these factors conspired against the highly accurate Norden bombsight. But all else being equal, there was no substitute for practical experience, and the USAAF

decided to press ahead and see for itself.

The ultra-high altitude bombing pioneered by the RAF in late 1941 was not repeated. Instead the American heavy bombers attacked in close formation from rather lower levels, relying on the

B-17 UNITS THAT BECAME OPERATIONAL IN ENGLAND 1942

Group No.	Squadrons	Base	First Mission	Notes
97	340, 341, 342, 414	Polebrook	17 Aug 42	to North Africa Nov 42
32	301, 352, 353, 419	Chelveston	5 Sept 42	to North Africa Nov 42
92	325, 326, 327, 407	Alconbury	Sept 42	training unit after four missions, returned to ops May 43 with YB-40.
306	367, 368, 369, 423	Thurleigh	9 Oct 42	Last mission 19 Apr 45
91	322, 323, 324, 401	Bassingbourn	7 Nov 42	Last mission 25 Apr 45
303	358, 359, 369, 427	Molesworth	17 Nov 42	Last mission 25 Apr 45
305	364, 365, 366, 422	Grafton Underwood	17 Nov 42	Last mission 25 Apr 45

Above: The Yanks are coming! Fortresses on Iceland, 21 July 1942.

The first unit to arrive in England was the 97th BG, equipped with B-17Es; it was followed by other units with the newer B-17F. The recently formed US 8th Air Force had received its first weapons. Intensive training followed, and a period of acclimatization to European weather conditions.

The first mission was flown by the 97th BG, which was based at Polebrook, on 17 August 1942. Twelve B-17Es raided the Sotteville marshalling yards at Rouen, strongly escorted by four RAF Spitfire squadrons. Visibility was good, and about half the bombs landed in the target area. Two bombers were slightly damaged by flak. It was a promising

Below: Early loss. A Fortress breaks up and goes down over northern France after being hit on the way to the target. (USAF)

Above: **They're here! Two B-17F Fortresses of the 91st BG arrive in England late in 1942. In the foreground are a Hurricane (left) and a Fairchild Argus (right) of the RAF. (Merle Olmsted)**

debut, and all seemed set fair for the 8th AF, with the 301st BG in pre-combat training and the 92nd BG arriving. Due shortly were the 306th, 91st, 303rd and 305th BGs.

The 97th was given no time to rest on its laurels. Two dozen B-17Es bombed Abbeville airfield on 19 August during the Dieppe Raid, and the next day 12 aircraft attacked the Amiens marshalling yards, again with a Spitfire escort. All the bombers returned unscathed on both occasions, having seen little of German fighters.

Shallow penetrations over enemy territory continued for the rest of the month; sometimes the bombing was accurate, at others it was less so. In September the 301st and 92nd BGs became operational, and joined the fray. Then on 6 September, the Luftwaffe reacted strongly, penetrated the escorting fighters and shot down two of the 20 B-17s. The loss of 10 per cent of the raiding force came as a nasty shock.

In November, just as the B-17 force was getting into its stride, the 97th and 301st BGs were transferred to the 12th Air Force in North Africa, while the

92nd BG became a B-17 'finishing school', and did not return to action until September of the following year. This left only the 306th BG in the front line, although it was joined during the month by the 91st, 303rd and 305th BGs. The latter two units flew their first mission on 17 November.

It was not an auspicious start. The target was the U-boat base at St Nazaire, but it was obscured by heavy cloud. Those that managed to bomb were met with fierce flak, though they all returned. The 303rd had no such luck. They completely failed to find the target, and brought their bombs home. On the following day, the 303rd managed to bomb St Nazaire. The problem was that the

briefed target was La Pallice, over 100 miles (160km) away! This was the very thing that daylight raiding was supposed to avoid. Then, four days later, only 11 out of 76 bombers despatched were able to find Lorient.

The final months of 1942 were very much a proving period for the B-17 units. Methods and tactics were in a continual state of flux. Formations were changed in an attempt to use the heavy defensive armament to its best advantage, while allowing concentrated bombing. The leader in this field was Colonel Curtis LeMay, commanding the 305th BG at Chelveston. One of the problems to be overcome was that of bomb aiming. It was impossible to keep a tight formation yet still have every aircraft aim individually, without risking multiple mid-air collisions. Having sorted out his optimum formation, LeMay solved the aiming problem by having everyone drop when they saw the leader's bombs go down. Sophisticated it was not, but against all but pinpoint targets it was good enough, and at least it ensured concentration. As 1942 drew to a close, the 8th had neither raided Germany nor attempted a deep penetration so far. But this was not far off.

■ 1943 ■
THE TEMPO INCREASES

The Casablanca Directive, signed on 21 January 1943, listed target types in

Below: **The 91st BG returns to base at Bassingbourn after a sortie. (USAF)**

REVISED 18-AIRCRAFT GROUP DEC 1942

The revised 18-aircraft Bomb Group formation, introduced in December 1942. The requirements were threefold; a concentrated bomb pattern which called for a narrow frontage; concentration of defensive firepower, which called for close formation, and freedom from masking the defensive guns, which demanded vertical staggering of aircraft. Formations changed throughout the course of the war, culminating in 1945 with a 36-aircraft BG occupying a frontage of 1,170ft (356m), with four nine-aircraft squadrons staggered through 1,150ft (350m) vertically.

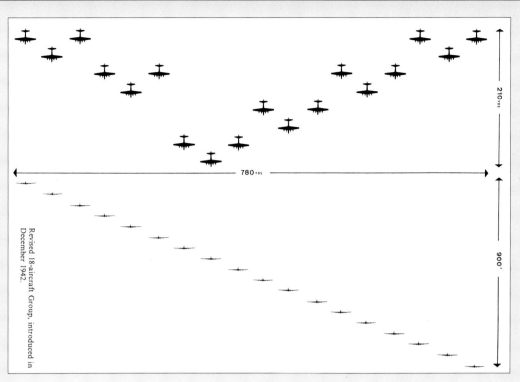

Revised 18-aircraft Group, introduced in December 1942.

order of priority. They were: U-boat construction; aircraft construction; transport; fuel; other industries. Six days later, the 8th AF put this into practice as 67 B-17s set off to raid the U-boat construction yards at Vegesack, the first German target scheduled.

As was so often the case, the primary target was socked in by cloud, and the

The 8th AF begins its assault on Germany

secondary, which was Wilhelmshaven, was attacked instead, although with unimpressive results. Fortunately the flak was ineffective, and the FW 190 pilots of JG. 1, lacking experience in estimating range against anything as large as a B-17, failed to press home their attacks. Three

Right: A tight 'ladder' of bombs goes down from a B-17F of the 96th BG. In the background are other groups in rather ragged formations, while flak bursts stain the sky. (Boeing via Alfred Price)

bombers were shot down for 22 German fighters claimed, which seemed a good rate of exchange.

Appalling weather foiled planned raids on Germany over the next few months, while the Luftwaffe fighters polished their tactics and became ever more effective. Although much of the early bombing effort was directed against the U-boats, it quickly became apparent that measures against the fighters were badly needed. In the largest raid so far, 115 B-17s took off on 17 April, their

target the Focke-Wulf factory at Bremen.

Fighters arrived in force as the bombing run commenced, and wave after wave of them attacked from head-on. The leading wing, consisting of the 91st and 306th BGs, suffered the worst of the onslaught. In the former the entire low squadron went down, while the latter lost 10 out of 16 aircraft. Total losses for the mission were 16; one to flak, the rest to fighters. This amounted to 14 per cent of the entire force, while another 48 bombers returned with varying

54-AIRCRAFT COMBAT WING FORMATION INTRODUCED MARCH 1943

The 54-aircraft Combat Wing, consisting of three Bomb Groups each of 18 aircraft, was introduced in March 1943. Its aims were basically those of the Bomb Group formation; bombing concentration and defensive security. At first it occupied a box of sky some 1¹/₃ miles (2km) wide, 1,800ft (550m) from front to rear, and 2,900ft (880m) vertically. This proved unwieldy, and it was condensed into just over ¹/₂ mile (900m) wide, 1,275ft (390m) front to rear, and 2,700ft (820m) vertically.

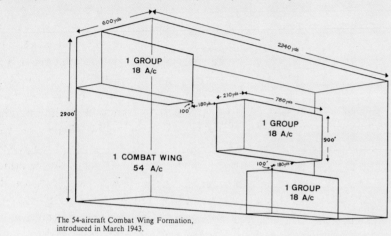

The 54-aircraft Combat Wing Formation, introduced in March 1943.

GUNNER CLAIMS

Overclaiming has always been a feature of air warfare, and arises from confusion caused by the rapidity of events. This was inevitable. Several dozen gunners blazed away at one fighter; if it went down they all claimed it in good faith. Even the most expert debriefer could not sort out the tangle with any degree of accuracy. Figures for the period allowed 450 claims for fighters destroyed to be upheld, but the true figure was in all probability fewer than 50. Total bomber losses for the same period amounted to 103. The false picture thus presented gave rise to unfounded optimism in the USAAF.

Escort fighters were desperately needed. The British Spitfire was too short-legged for the task; the Republic P-47 Thunderbolt was better, but not by much, while the twin-engined Lockheed P-38 Lightning was no match for the agile Focke-Wulfs and Messerschmitts in a dogfight. It was at this point that the 92nd BG returned to operations, bringing with them the YB-40 gunship, of which so much was hoped. As related previously, these were a failure and were withdrawn from service in September of that year.

On 22 June came the deepest penetration yet when 235 Fortresses raided the synthetic rubber plant at Huls, in the Ruhr. To minimize fighter opposition, a feint course was flown to deceive the German fighter controllers, while both

Right: **Not all losses were attributable to enemy action. A B-17F of the 91st BG sheds its load without realizing that another aircraft has strayed almost directly beneath it. The first bomb strikes the tailplane without detonating, bending it down. In the final picture the unfortunate Fortress goes down out of control; the victim of poor lookout and less than perfect station-keeping. (Boeing via Alfred Price)**

the RAF and USAAF mounted diversionary operations. This worked in part, but one of the diversionary forces suffered heavily. The main force landed just under 25 per cent of their bombs on target, which was a good result for the time. The plant was out of action for a month and production reduced for five months thereafter. Sixteen Fortresses of the main force failed to return, a more acceptable 6.8 per cent, one of them a YB-40 hit by flak, but no fewer than 170 were damaged.

The weather improved in late July, and a series of heavy raids was made by forces of 250–300 bombers. The deeper penetrations were often combined with raids on targets in occupied Europe by medium bombers, splitting the defender's strength. Then on 28 July, bombers returning from Oschersleben beset by German fighters were met at the Dutch border by more than 100 P-47s equipped

degrees of damage. This rate of attrition could not be sustained. The one apparent bright spot was the claim for 63 German fighters destroyed, but this turned out to be misleading.

celebrated with the most ambitious deep penetration yet. Early that morning, 147 Fortresses took off to attack the Messerschmitt works at Regensburg, escorted by Thunderbolts as far as the German border. Shortly after, another 230 B-17s would take off, bound for the ball-bearing factories at Schweinfurt. These had no escort, as the German fighters would be on the ground refuelling and rearming. At least, that was how it was planned. In the event the second wave was delayed by fog, and got away hours later.

The German fighters waited for the Thunderbolts to turn back before launching their attack on the first wave. Then dozens of single and twin-engined fighters pounced. For the next 90 minutes they tore into the bombers, concentrating on the rearmost bombardment wing, which lost 13 Fortresses. Four more went down from the two leading wings. Only as the target hove in sight did the attacks cease. Visibility was excellent, and the bombing, led by Curtis LeMay, was accurate. The force then veered to the southwest, crossed Italy, and landed in North Africa, the first of the so-called 'shuttle' missions. On arrival, 24 B-17s were missing; one had crash-landed in Italy; two more, badly damaged, had sought sanctuary in Switzerland, while four had ditched in the Mediterranean out of fuel. Refuelled and rearmed, the German fighters waited in vain for the return flight.

They were however rewarded by the arrival of the second wave, now three

The 8th AF lose 60 bombers against Regensburg and Schweinfurt

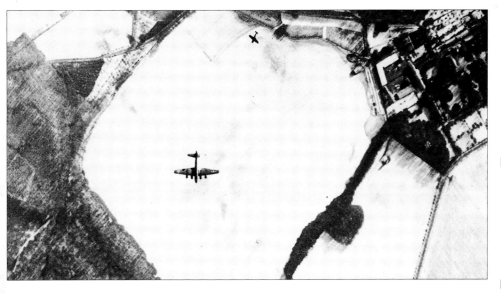

Top: **Lockheed P-38 Lightnings escorting Fortresses of the 381st BG late in 1943. (USAF)**
Above: **Flames streaming from the starboard wing and separated from its formation, a Fortress is remorselessly hunted down by a FW 190 after raiding the aircraft plant at Oschersleben. (USAF)**

with new drop tanks to extend their radius of action. These shot down nine of their assailants in short order. It was the shape of things to come.

■ SCHWEINFURT ■

It was 17 August 1943, the anniversary of the raid on Rouen, and the event was

hours behind schedule. This time they concentrated on the leading bombardment wing. Twenty-one bombers were shot down by fighters on the way to Schweinfurt and one more was lost to flak over the target. The second wave did not head for North Africa; instead it returned to England, losing 14 more en

Above: Aircraft of the 381st BG lined up on the runway at Ridgewell prior to a mission. (USAF)

route. Schweinfurt was heavily hit, although accuracy was less than had been achieved at Regensburg.

Losses on this two-pronged raid were 60 Fortresses lost on the day, or 16 per cent. But worse was to come. When the remnants of the first wave returned from Tunisia, it was without 55 bombers too badly damaged to make the return flight. In all, the raid cost 118 aircraft, an unacceptable attrition rate of 31 per cent. American gunners claimed an incredible 288 fighters destroyed, later reduced to 148. Actual German fighter losses were just 25. Nor was the damage on the ground particularly rewarding. Production resumed a few days later, and was normal after a few weeks.

■ BOMBING THROUGH ■ THE WEATHER

The weeks following the Schweinfurt raid were quiet, with shallow penetrations only, as losses were made good. The B-17G started arriving in England at about this time, ready for its combat debut. The 8th did not sally forth in force again until 6 September, when 338 Fortresses set out for Stuttgart. This time the main enemy was the weather. Heavy cloud covered much of Western Europe,

Right: A Messerschmitt 110 curves away after attacking Fortresses of the 91st BG. (USAF)

Stuttgart was socked in and few so much as saw it; formation cohesion was lost. German fighters attacked in force over the target area, and again near Paris on the return flight. The result was a disaster. Eleven B-17s were lost to fighters; a round dozen came down in the Channel out of fuel; at least two more crashed on landing, while five lost or damaged machines set down in Switzerland. All this with hardly a bomb anywhere near the target.

The weather was kind to Germany over the following weeks, and the remainder of the month passed with raids on French and Belgian objectives. On 15 September two 1,000lb (450kg) bombs were carried on racks externally for the first time, one of the rare occasions on which this was done. Meanwhile, measures to overcome the worst effects of cloud were in hand.

In August 1943, the 482nd Bomb Group was formed at Alconbury, as the 8th Air Force's sole Pathfinder unit. It was made up of two B-17 and one B-24 squadrons equipped with British gadgets. The first was Gee, a comparatively short-ranged navigational device. The second was Oboe which, using signals from English ground stations, allowed fairly accurate blind bombing. The third was H_2S, a primitive (by modern standards) ground mapping radar, later slightly improved to become H_2X. The former was carried in a bathtub under the chin, the latter initially in a retractable dome in the same position, although production aircraft had this fitted in place of the ball turret. All Pathfinder aircraft carried smoke markers. Dropped above a solid undercast on radar indications alone, these left a distinctive trail above the clouds obscuring the target, providing a point at which successive waves of bombers could aim.

Pathfinding with H_2S was pioneered on 27 September with an attack on

SCHWEINFURT

'I watched two fighters explode not far beneath, disappearing in sheets of orange flame, B-17s dropping out in every state of distress, from engines on fire to control surfaces shot away, friendly and enemy parachutes floating down and, on the green carpet far beneath us, numerous funeral pyres of smoke from fallen aircraft, marking our trail.'

COL. BEIRNE LAY

Emden. The leading Wing dropped with the Pathfinder aircraft; the second Wing dropped on the smoke markers, while the third was able to find a gap in the cloud and bombed visually. Post-strike reconnaissance showed that only the Pathfinder-led units had hit Emden; the visual bombers were miles adrift. It was a promising start. A blind bombing leader was to become a standard part of most 8th AAF raids. But first the technique had to be refined, and sufficient crews trained.

In 1943, the life expectancy of a Fortress was a mere 11 missions; a tour of duty was 25 missions. When a crewman completed his tour – and a surprising number did – he was statistically dead twice over! However, progress was being made. Carpet, a gunlaying radar jammer, gradually entered service, and this equipment decreased the effectiveness of the flak. While flak destroyed only a small proportion of the bombers, it was responsible for most of those which returned damaged, while forcing them to bomb from ever higher altitudes, with a corresponding decrease in accuracy. Carpet was a British invention that saved many American lives.

The following month saw a return to Schweinfurt on the 14th by 291 Fortresses. As was by now standard procedure, the defending fighters held back until the bombers passed Aachen, when their escorts turned back. They then struck, in a way described by American official historians as 'unprecedented in its magnitude, in the cleverness with which it was planned, and in the severity with which it was executed'.

■ SCHWEINFURT ■ AGAIN!

By the time that Schweinfurt was reached, 28 bombers had gone down and many others were badly damaged. Despite this, the bombing was heavy and

Above: A direct hit by heavy flak has torn the front fuselage and port inner engine clean away from this B-17, which goes down blazing furiously. (USAF)

accurate, and only one aircraft was lost to flak in the target area. But now they had to run the fighter gauntlet once more on the homeward leg. Again they were assailed from all sides, and by the time that they reached the relative safety of the escorts, formations were breaking up, all cohesion lost.

Three ball-bearing factories had been hard hit, but once again the price was high. Sixty Fortresses were lost; five more crashed on reaching England, and 12 were written off with battle damage; over 26 per cent of the total. A further 121 were damaged but repairable. Barely one in every three returned unscathed, and these figures might have been still worse had it not been that the RAF sent fighters with long-range tanks to the aid of the hard-pressed American Thunderbolt and Lightning escorts.

The defenders had taken the measure of the Fortresses. They used 21cm rockets to break up the closely packed bomber formations, then attacked en masse from head-on. The B-17 was a tough bird, able to sustain severe damage and keep flying, and it normally took several attacks on one machine to bring it down. The essential thing, from the German point of view, was to isolate it so that it could be picked off at leisure.

The second Schweinfurt raid underlined what many had said all along; that unescorted bombers, no matter how well armed, could not fly daylight missions against determined fighter opposition without incurring unacceptable losses. The price was too high; long-range escort fighters were needed more desperately than ever.

Using drop tanks, P-47s were able to penetrate a little way into Germany; P-38s a bit further. Then in December came the answer to the problem. The P-51 Mustang was a happy marriage of an American airframe and a British engine. Using drop tanks it could range deep into Germany and go all the way to most targets.

■ BIG WEEK ■
AND BERLIN

Operations continued following the Schweinfurt raid, but increasingly poor weather meant that many of them were radar bombing missions led by Pathfinders. Few visual attacks could be made, and in January 1944 the 8th concentrated mainly on V-1 launch sites in the Pas-de-Calais. Not until late February did the bombers really get into their stride again, as the clouds parted, giving clear skies over Germany.

Big Week, the period from 20 to 25 February, saw a concerted attempt by the Allies to cripple the German aircraft industry. At last with escort fighters able to accompany them, the bombers raided Focke-Wulf plants at Tuetow and Oschersleben; Messerschmitt factories at Augsburg, Regensburg, Gotha, Brunswick, Furth and Erla/Leipzig; the Junkers works at Bernberg, Aschersleben and Halberstadt; and Heinkel's facility at Rostock. Immediate German production losses were estimated at 1,000 aircraft, and many more over the next few months. Total bomber losses, B-17s and B-24s, amounted to 226; just under 6 per cent of the 3,800 sorties flown. Fighter escort losses during Big Week amounted to 28, but the low figure of bomber loss underlined their worth.

On 4 March, the bombers set off to

B-17 UNITS THAT BECAME OPERATIONAL ENGLAND 1943

Group No.	Squadrons	Base	First Mission	Notes
94	331, 332, 333, 410	Bassingbourn	13 May 43	Last mission 21 Apr 45
95	334, 335, 336, 412	Alconbury	13 May 43	Last mission 20 Apr 45
96	337, 338, 339, 413	Grafton Underwood	14 May 43	Last mission 21 Apr 45
351	508, 509, 510, 511	Polebrook	14 May 43	Last mission 25 Apr 45. Film star Clark Gable flew with this group
379	524, 525, 526, 527	Kimbolton	29 May 43	Last mission 25 Apr 45; flew most sorties, dropped greatest bomb tonnage.
381	532, 533, 534, 535	Ridgewell	22 Jun 43	Last mission 25 Apr 45
384	544, 545, 546, 547	Grafton Underwood	22 Jun 43	Last mission 25 Apr 45, dropped last 8th AF bombs of war
100	349, 350, 351, 418	Podington	25 Jun 43	Last mission 20 Apr 45
385	548, 549, 550, 551	Gt Ashfield	17 Jul 43	Last mission 20 Apr 45
388	560, 561, 562, 563	Knettishall	17 Jul 43	Last mission April 45, flew 19 Aphrodite missions
389	568, 569, 570, 571	Framlingham	27 Sep 43	Last mission 20 Apr 45
482	812, 813, third sqn flew B-24s	Alconbury	27 Sep 43	Last mission 22 Mar 44, pioneer Pathfinder unit, also operational research
410	612, 613, 614, 615	Deenethorpe	26 Nov 43	Last mission Apr 45
447	708, 709, 710, 711	Rattlesden	24 Dec 43	Last mission 21 Apr 45

NB: The 422 BS commenced operations as part of 305 BG in Nov 42; then pioneered night bombing for 8th AF in Sep/Oct 43. Night leaflet sqn from 7/8 Oct 43. Based at Chelveston, redesignated 858 BS in June 44, re-equipped with B-24s the following month.

marker. They were intercepted on the homeward leg, but the Mustang escorts fought heroically to protect them, losing 23 of their number. Five Fortresses failed to return, a surprisingly small loss under the circumstances.

Two days later the 8th tried again. The force consisted of 561 Fortresses, tasked against a ball-bearing factory in the Erkner suburb and against the Bosch factory at Klein Machnow, plus 249 Liberators which were to attack the Daimler-Benz engine works. Fighter cover was provided by 691 Thunderbolts, Lightnings and Mustangs, some of the latter RAF, working in relays. The distance to Berlin ensured that no deceptive course changes could be used; the German fighters would have plenty of time to deploy.

Such a force could not be hidden. The time-consuming process of assembling such a massive armada in its correct order meant that it was under radar observation long before it left the English coast. In the occupied countries and in Germany, fighter units were brought to readiness; on this day they were to meet numbers with numbers.

The bomber stream was 94 miles (150km) long, thundering eastwards at 180mph (290km/hr), but some four hours after the first bomber had taken

Top: H₂X ground mapping radar, fitted in a retractable dome in the nose compartment, allowed blind bombing through cloud. This was an experimental installation.
Above: Radar-equipped pathfinder of the 401st BG, showing the retractable radome fitted in place of the ball turret. (Ralph Trout)
Right: A heavily armed Messerschmitt Me 410 commences its firing pass on a B-17F of the 390th BG.

Berlin, the only major German target not yet attacked in daylight. Once again the weather turned sour, and the recall signal was issued, but one combat wing of 29 Fortresses failed to receive it and carried on. Realizing this, headquarters allowed part of the escort to continue also. Fighters were encountered as the bombers neared the target, but they pressed on, releasing their loads on a Pathfinder's

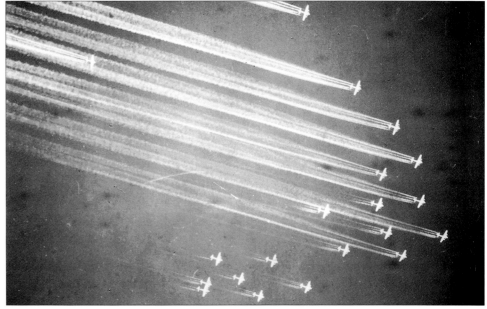

Above: Long-range escort fighters wheel protectively above B-17F Fortresses of the 390th BG. They tipped the balance against the defenders decisively. (USAF via Alfred Price)

Right: Flying Fortresses over the German capital. The low squadron is barely in the contrail belt. (USAF)

off, it had become disorganized. The head of the stream, well protected by Thunderbolts, had inadvertently veered southwards. The 13th Combat Wing was running behind schedule, and had lost visual contact with the aircraft in front. Not realizing this, it continued on the correct course, thus forming an offset in the formation.

The first German fighters attacked over Haselunne, just east of the Dutch border, to meet the 13th CW head-on. Only eight Thunderbolts were on hand to greet 107 Me 109s and FW 190s, and this was not enough to hold them off. The German fighters flashed between the bombers, guns blazing, and narrowly avoided collisions with them. Damaged Fortresses dropped out of formation in all directions; easy meat for the waiting fighters as they swung round to re-engage. Black smoke from burning aircraft stained the clear sky; white parachutes blossomed below.

Calls for help brought more P-47s from all directions; these took some of the pressure off, but there were simply not enough of them. The unengaged German fighters regrouped for another head-on attack. In all the battle lasted 45 minutes.

Above: Target Berlin! Tempelhof airfield can be seen near the right wingtip of this 452nd BG Fortress as it lines up on its primary target. (USAF)

Meanwhile the front of the bomber stream was faring almost as badly. Attempting to get back on course, it crossed several flak zones before meeting up with another huge German fighter formation. The escorting Mustangs were in the right place, but failed to avert the blow completely. More bombers went down, although the German interceptors paid a heavy price for their success.

At last the bombers reached Berlin, only to run into the most vicious flak that most of them had ever seen. Partial cloud foiled the bomb runs on two of the primary three targets but widespread damage was caused in the city. The return flight was marked by skirmishes with small numbers of German fighters, which were generally held at bay by the escorts. There was however one exception. Forty-four German fighters managed to assemble near the Dutch border; they cost the 388th BG six Fortresses.

Losses on the Berlin raid amounted to 73, of which 56 were Fortresses. Of these, three reached Sweden in a damaged state, while four were struck off charge in England. Fighters accounted for 45, fighters and flak for four; flak alone for six, while one fell to unknown causes. This was the largest bomber loss ever suffered in one raid by the 8th Air Force. However, it was not enough to stop the 8th. Over the next three days, two raids of similar strength were visited upon the German capital, and a third on 22 March.

With the invasion of Europe looming, priorities switched. Attacks against communications centres intensified, while tremendous efforts were made to reduce

The 8th prepare for invasion; oil and transport the targets

the German oil industry. On 12 May, 935 heavy bombers raided oil plants at Bruex, Bohlen, Leuna, Lutzendorf and Zwickau. Meanwhile 15th Air Force was raiding the Romanian oil fields at Ploesti. Raid followed raid, and aviation fuel production slumped from 175,000 tons in April to 52,000 tons in June; 35,000 tons in July, and a mere 7,000 tons in September. This caused a tremendous reduction of German fighter effectiveness.

Below: A large hole through her fin making control difficult, *Boche Buster* of the 401st BG breaks formation to seek safety in neutral Sweden, 7 October 1944. (Bert Hocking)

FORTRESSES THROUGH THE BERLIN FLAK

'A dark puffy veil that hung like a pall of death covered the capital city. It was the heaviest flak I had ever seen. It almost seemed to swallow up the bomber formations as they entered it. One ship blew up and three others dropped away from their formations . . . It didn't seem that anything could fly through that. But there they were, Flying Fortresses sailing proudly away from the scene of devastation.'

LT LOWELL WATTS, 388TH BG.

By October 1944 the bombing campaign against the Third Reich had sapped the strength of the German day fighter arm. Lack of aircraft was not the cause; widely dispersed plants scattered throughout Germany maintained production at record levels, and the depots were full of replacements.

The critical shortage was of trained pilots. Under the constant battering of the massive American raids, which were increasingly covered by long-range escorts, the German fighter units had suffered swingeing losses. Experienced men were irreplaceable; novices rarely lasted long. Then, as the fuel shortage bit ever harder, training was curtailed, and the quality of replacement pilots dropped still more. To make matters worse, even the ever-shrinking band of old stagers sometimes found themselves grounded for lack of fuel. From this time on, only on rare occasions were they able to put up serious opposition to the American armadas. Fortress operations over Germany gradually became safer, so much so that in the closing months of the war it was possible to fly a full tour and never encounter a German fighter in the air! On the other hand, the flak defences were strengthened, and losses to this cause began to exceed those of the fighters, although without reaching anywhere near the same proportions. This reduction in risk was acknowledged by the USAAF, who increased the number of sorties in a tour of operations from 25 to 30, and eventually to 35.

While in the early months the loss rate of Fortresses was horrendous, a few, and they were very few indeed, survived to complete more than 100 missions. Yet others had taken such a beating that they were no longer sufficiently reliable for operations, although still flyable. One

Left: The 91st BG unloads over Berlin on smoke markers dropped by lead aircraft in February 1945. The nearest aircraft is a late model B-17G, with the taller dorsal turret. (USAF)

use for some of these was as assembly ships. Shuffling a formation of many hundreds of bombers into the correct order before sallying forth was far from easy. One solution was to paint war-weary aircraft in brilliant colours and strange patterns. These unmistakeable psychedelic monsters were then launched and took up their assigned place in the assembly area, where their assigned formations took station on them. When all was in order, they returned to base.

■ **APHRODITE** ■

Another use for war-weary B-17s was as radio-controlled flying bombs. Stripped of all unnecessary equipment, these were packed with 20,000lb (9,000kg) of Torpex high explosive. For Project Aphrodite, as it was known, these were flown off by a two-man crew, who parachuted to safety near the English coast. Control was then handed over to a specially equipped 'mother' aircraft, which remotely guided the flying bomb to its target. The hazardous Aphrodite

Above: Mustangs escort B-17G *Patches* on a 15th AF shuttle mission to Russia. The long reach of the American fighter transformed American deep penetration missions. (USAF)

missions were flown by the 388th BG from Fersfield, an isolated airfield in the wilds of Norfolk, but the difficulties of accurately guiding them onto their targets, plus a couple of unfortunate accidents, ensured that only a handful of missions were flown.

Other experiments carried out from

B-17 UNITS THAT BECAME OPERATIONAL IN ENGLAND, 1944

Group	Squadrons	Base	1st Mission	Notes
	803	Oulton	5 Jun 44	Countermeasures Squadron, 8 B-17Fs and 2 B-17Gs. Largely replaced by B-24s from August 44.
486	832, 833, 834, 835	Sudbury	1 Aug 44	Last mission 21 Apr 45. (prev B-24s)
487	836, 837, 938, 839	Lavenham	1 Aug 44	Last mission 21 Apr 45. (prev B-24s)
490	848, 849, 850, 851	Eye	27 Aug 44	Last mission 20 Apr 45. (prev B-24s)
493	860, 861, 862, 863	Debach	8 Sep 44	(prev B-24s) Last mission 20 Apr 45. Last BG to become operational in 8th AF.
25 (R)	652 Sqn only with B-17, others with B-24	Watton	Nov 44	Composite unit, weather reconnaissance.
34	4, 7, 18, 391	Mendlesham	17 Sep 44	(prev B-24s) No losses to fighters over enemy territory.

Left: The 30mm cannon of the Messerschmitt Me 262 jet fighter packed a tremendous punch. This Fortress was lucky to survive. (USAF via Alfred Price)
Below left: In the final months of the war flak was the main hazard. On 10 April 1945, *Wee Willie* of the 91st BG went down on its 124th sortie. (USAF via Alfred Price)

remarkably low; less than one-third of a per cent. One B-17 was lost to a Me 262 jet fighter, while four more went down to flak, which damaged a further 85 aircraft. Just to show it was no fluke, 1,193 heavies went out on the following day, losing only two of their number. The pattern continued.

Whereas the British Lancaster routinely carried bombs of up to 12,000lb (5,400kg), Fortress (and Liberator) bays could not accommodate a bomb larger than 2,000lb (900kg). This was of little use against hardened targets, and the Disney bomb was introduced to correct this shortcoming. Weighing 4,500lb (2,000kg), it used rocket propulsion to pierce 20ft (6m) of reinforced concrete.

Nine B-17s of the 92 BG each carried four Disney bombs on underwing racks to the U-boat pens at Ijmuiden on 14 March 1945. Only one hit was scored, and a further raid was mounted, but

Fersfield involved Batty, a system using a television-guided bomb. Rather ahead of its time, Batty was beset with technical difficulties, and achieved little.

To return to the bombing of Germany, some idea of the reduction of defensive effectiveness was given on 22 February 1945, when 1,411 heavy bombers attacked communication centres all over the Third Reich from the unprecedentedly low altitude of 10,000ft (3,050m), chosen to achieve bombing accuracy against small targets. Losses were

Above right: Not all losses were fatal. Damaged by fighters, this B-17G of the 96th BG force-landed in Denmark. Aided by the Resistance, the entire crew escaped to Sweden. (J. Helme via Alfred Price)
Right: B-17F *Talisman*, seen here at Port Moresby in 1943, was one of the last B-17s to operate in the Pacific theatre. (USAF)

soon the Allied advance overran the area, making further attacks unnecessary.

Just four days later, the 8th mounted its final major attack on Berlin with 1,327 heavy bombers. They were met by an estimated 40–50 Me 262 jet fighters, which accounted for a mere eight Fortresses. The remaining 16 bombers which failed to return, plus a further 16 which force-landed in Russian-held territory, all fell to flak. The loss rate of three percent, while heavy for 1945, was a far cry from the first Berlin raid just over a year earlier.

Final rounds In Europe; operations continue in the Pacific

By now worthwhile targets were becoming few and far between, and on 16 April, General Spaatz stated that the strategic air war was over; from then on only tactical targets remained. The final 8th AF bombs of the war were dropped on the Skoda Armament Works at Pilsen on 25 April 1945, by a B-17 of the 384th BG.

B-17 OPERATIONAL STATISTICS 8TH AF

BG No.	Missions	Sorties	Bombs	A/c Missing	Sort/Miss (tons)
303	364	10,721	24,918	165	64.98
306	342	9,614	22,575	171	56.22
91	340	9,591	22,142	197	48.68
305	337	9,231	22,363	154	59.94
379	330	10,492	26,460	141	74.41
94	324	8,884	18,925	153	58.06
95	320	8,903	19,769	157	56.70
96	320	8,924	19,277	189	47.21
384	314	9,348	22,415	159	58.79
351	311	8,600	20,357	124	69.35
92	308	8,663	20,829	154	56.25
100	306	8,630	19,257	177	48.78
388	306	8,051	18,162	142	56.70
390	300	8,725	19,059	144	60.59
381	296	9,035	22,160	131	68.97
385	296	8,264	18,494	129	64.06
447	257	7,605	17,103	97	78.40
410	255	7,430	17,778	95	78.21
452	250	7,279	16,467	110	66.17
457	237	7,068	16,916	83	85.16
398	195	6,419	15.781	58	110.67*
97	14	247	395	4	61.75
301	8	104	186	1	104.00
TOTALS	6,034	181,828	422,788	2,935	av61.95

1) At least four BGs converted from the B-24 to the B-17 in the summer of 1944, but their records include data for both aircraft, and have not been included here.

2) Missing aircraft are just that; no allowance has been made for those that reached base but crashed on landing, or were struck off charge. A rough approximation based on available sources gives about one-third as many again.

3) At one point early in the war, the life expectancy of a B-17 was just 11 sorties. The sorties/missing aircraft ratio shows how much safer things had become in the later stages. This is particularly noticeable with BGs formed late in 1944. Three factors were decisive; sufficient numbers of long-range escort fighters; from Spring 1944 many missions were flown over occupied France; in the final months of the war, the Luftwaffe was a spent force.

As by far the majority of Fortress operations in the Second World War were flown by the US 8th Army Air Force based in England, it was only to be expected that the narrative would mainly concern itself with these. But the B-17 served well and faithfully with other air forces and in other theatres.

We have already touched on the early years of the Pacific War. While those Fortresses there at the start gave sterling service, ably backed by such reinforcements as could be got through, this period was essentially tactical. There was little scope for strategic bombing until the Japanese advance had been halted, which did not happen until mid-1942. While the Fortresses helped to hold the ring, there was little more they could do. Vulnerable to fighters at medium and low altitudes, they yet lacked the precision to hit either small fixed targets or moving ships from high altitude.

This was all too clearly demonstrated at the decisive Battle of Midway in June 1942, when 19 B-17s were based on the island. During the four days of battle, they flew over 80 sorties in the course of seven missions. They first attacked the invasion force; the main Japanese carrier force twice; two cruisers; a solitary destroyer; and finally an American submarine under the impression that it was a Japanese cruiser. They claimed hits on two battleships or heavy cruisers; two transports; three aircraft carriers, and finally 'sank' the 'cruiser'. During this flurry of activity, two B-17s were lost. In actual fact there was not even a near-miss. The sunk 'cruiser' had of course crash-dived to safety.

Below: The Boeing B-29 Superfortress commenced operations in the Far East in June 1944, as B-17 production was being run down. (Author)